Writers and Writing
DEV: 042

Barbara Fine Clouse

with selected Chapters from
Working It Out
Third Edition

McGraw Hill Learning Solutions

Boston   Burr Ridge, IL   Dubuque, IA   New York   San Francisco   St. Louis
Bangkok   Bogotá   Caracas   Lisbon   London   Madrid
Mexico City   Milan   New Delhi   Seoul   Singapore   Sydney   Taipei   Toronto

Writers and Writing
DEV: 042
with Selected Chapters from Working It Out, Third Edition

1 2 3 4 5 6 7 8 9 0 QDB QDB 13 12 11

ISBN-13: 978-0-07-757793-3
ISBN-10: 0-07-757793-0

Learning Solutions Representative: Ann Hayes
Production Editor: Nichole Birkenholz
Printer/Binder: Quad/Graphics

Contents

The iDeal Reader

Clouse • *Cornerstones: Readings for Writers*

Clouse • *Cornerstones: Readings for Writers*

Acknowledgments

Sincere thanks to all of those who helped make this custom-published textbook possible: the Basic Writing students who submitted their essays for consideration; the Basic Writing faculty and peer tutors, who encouraged students to grow as writers; and the members of the essay selection committee—Nora Wagner, Cheryl Jamerson, Michelle Miller, Mindy Morse, and Becky McDonald–who gave generously of their time because they believe that student writing is a powerful tool for teaching and learning. Michelle Miller deserves special recognition as the Editor-in-Chief who also enthusiastically coordinated the essay selection committee, handled the paperwork, and prepared the material for publication.

Marjorie Keil
Basic Writing Coordinator

▶ WELCOME TO BASIC WRITING!

When starting a Basic Writing class, a student might say, "I'm taking this because I tested into it." However, at the end of the semester, in their course evaluations, the vast majority of students say something entirely different. They say that having the chance to begin college with Basic Writing is a great opportunity to learn and practice new habits for writing, to learn or relearn grammar rules, to make new friends, and to develop the strategies, skills, and self-image of a successful college writer.

If you practice good attendance and class participation, use the services of the Writing Lab regularly, do your work carefully, and turn it in on time, you, too, will be on your way to a successful experience in Basic Writing.

▶ REGARDING "QUESTIONS TO INSPIRE WRITING"

Note to students and instructors about using these questions: Use these questions not as checklists with boxes to be checked off but as springboards – something to bounce off into something daring and unexpected. You may also think of it this way—use these questions as pathways leading to discovery of yourself and bringing that discovery to a reader. Or look at it this way: as you write in response to these questions, think of yourself as a miner. You are not digging just to dig but to discover something, and until you do, you keep digging!

The University of Akron's

A Civil Climate for Learning: Statement of Expectations

The University of Akron is an educational community of diverse peoples, processes, and programs. While all of us have our individual backgrounds, outlooks, values, and styles, we all share certain principles of personal responsibility, mutual respect, and common decency. Our campus culture requires that we maintain and extend those principles, for without them, we cannot thrive as a humane and worthwhile university. To keep ourselves aware of these shared principles, this statement articulates some of the expectations and responsibilities of a civil climate for learning on our campus.

▶ PRINCIPLES OF OUR CAMPUS CULTURE

Our campus culture acknowledges the importance of all in our community for their participation in our common enterprise as a university. We value the contributions and we respect the needs of students, faculty, contract professionals, staff, administrators, maintenance and service personnel and everyone else whose work and dedication enables us to pursue our individual and collective goals.

Together, we maintain an **intellectual culture** that is accessible, disciplined, free, safe, and committed to excellence.

By our behavior and with one another, we endorse a culture of diversity, celebrating the uniqueness of the individual and developing our understanding and tolerance of differences in gender, ethnicity, age, spiritual belief, sexual orientation, and physical or mental potential.

We take responsibility for sustaining a **caring culture**, nurturing growth and fulfillment in one another and in the larger communities of which we are a part.

We insist on a **culture of civility**, united in our rejections of violence, coercion, deceit, or terrorism. We work to increase collaboration, cooperation, and consensus within rational dialogue characterized by mutual respect and consideration.

Ours is a **responsible culture**. We expect each member of our community to carry out responsibly his or her duties for preserving the integrity, quality, and decency of our environment and our discourse.

► EXPECTATIONS AND RESPONSIBILITIES

To preserve and promote the culture of The University of Akron, everyone must engage in certain specific behaviors. Anyone new to this campus must be aware of the expectations we have of each other and be committed to fulfilling his/her responsibility in maintaining our culture.

► INSIDE THE CLASSROOM

Inside the classroom, **faculty** are expected to respect the sanctity of the teaching/learning process by honoring their commitment to students in terms of time, fairness, and enthusiasm. It is the responsibility of faculty to set and enforce the classroom rules of conduct. Faculty members are expected to treat men and women, persons of all colors and ethnicities, and persons with varying abilities, spiritual preferences, or sexual orientation with equitable respect and consideration.

Students are expected to respect the sanctity of the teaching/learning process by expressing respect for the faculty member as the organizer and guide through this learning experience as well as for fellow students. Disruptive, disrespectful, discriminatory, harassing, violent behavior is explicitly prohibited. Academic dishonesty will not be tolerated. Students are expected to take responsibility for their own learning and, in return, can expect responsible teaching from the faculty member. Students should report unprofessional behavior on the part of faculty members. Students have a right to expect that they will not be sexually or otherwise harassed, intimidated, or threatened.

► ON THE CAMPUS

On the campus, everyone is expected to respect and protect the dignity and freedom of each other. There must be the opportunity for expression of all points of view, free from name-calling or ridicule. All members of the University family are expected to be civil and tolerant of others. It is the responsibility of each member of the University community to express dissatisfaction with anyone who fails to meet the responsibility of civility and to request that they do so. In the event that cooperation cannot be attained, proper authorities must be involved to insist upon these minimum expectations. Only by campus-wide compliance to these expectations can we achieve a clear sense of our campus culture and, accordingly, a sense of mutual pride.

Students can expect that all representation of all departmental and administrative offices will treat them with respect, a sense of cooperation and with concern for their welfare. Students can also expect appropriate coordination of services among departments.

Everyone is expected to respect the campus environment by behaving in ways that protect the safety, order and appearance of all campus facilities. Each person must take steps to preserve the ecological and aesthetic aspects of the campus.

▶ ADDITIONAL BEHAVIORAL EXPECTATIONS

All members of the University community are required to abide by all laws and regulations of The University of Akron, the City of Akron, the State of Ohio, and the Federal Government. Students are expected to abide by the Student Code of Conduct and the University Disciplinary Procedures. Faculty, contract professionals, administrators, and staff are expected to abide by all University regulations and procedures.

What Does It Take to Become a Successful College-Level Writer?

Since many students in Basic Writing have been out of school for a while or have had limited experience with writing, the course has been designed to provide an opportunity for them to learn what it means to be a college-level writer. What is a college-level writer? The following questions, if answered with a *yes*, indicate that the student is ready to begin the process of becoming a college-level writer.

1. Can you keep up and get drafts in on time?
2. Can you discipline yourself to come to class—on time—four hours a week?
3. Do you know how to reach the instructor when you need to be absent or when you have a question between classes?
4. Can you discipline yourself to work with a Writing Lab tutor several times during the semester?
5. Do you understand that the reading assignments must be read more than once in order to grasp the writer's intended meaning?
6. Do you realize that it takes practice over several weeks to understand what a college-level essay is—and that it takes more than one draft to write one?
7. Are you able to discipline yourself to avoid procrastinating or leaving out steps in the writing process?
8. Do you realize that for every 4 hours spent in class each week you are expected to spend 6-8 hours outside of class on homework?
9. Do you believe that the instructor is interested in your academic growth and that the course has been designed to prepare you to write in college?
10. Do you believe that it is worth your effort to complete all of the assignments?
11. Do you understand that having your own textbooks and bringing them to class is essential and that borrowing textbooks from other students—especially to take the in-class quizzes—is unacceptable?

Thanks to BW instructor, Gayle King

The University of Akron

Student Resources for Academic and Personal Support

The University of Akron is dedicated to laying the foundation for all of our students' success and personal growth

> ▷ in the **learning environment**,
> ▷ in the **campus community**, and
> ▷ in the larger, **diverse world**, ...**through**...
> ▷ **quality instruction** by **dedicated faculty**,
> ▷ opportunities for **campus and community engagement**, and
> ▷ a **supportive environment**.

Academic Advising	**Academic Advisement Center**, Simmons Hall 205, 330-972-7430
	Buchtel College of Arts and Sciences, Dean's Office, CAS 448, 330-972-7880
	College of Business Administration, Advising, CBA 260, 330-972-7042
	College of Creative and Professional Arts, Dean's Office, Guzzetta 260, 330-972-7564
	College of Education, Advising, Zook 207, 330-972-6970
	College of Engineering, Dean's Office, ASEC 201, 330-972-7816
	College of Health Sciences and Human Services, Dean's Office, Guzzetta 260, 330-972-7564
	College of Nursing, Student Affairs, MGH 313, 330-972-5103
	Honors College, Honors Complex 178, 330-972-7966
	Summit College Advising, Polsky 301, 330-972-7220
Adult Students	**UA Adult Focus**, Adult Learner Services, Schrank Hall North 260, 330-972-5793, **www.uakron.edu/uaaf**
Bookstores	**Barnes and Noble**, Student Union, 1st Floor, 330-972-7624; Polsky Bldg, 3rd Floor, 330-972-8166; **www.uakron.bncollege.com**
Child Care	**Center for Child Development** (child care for 18 months-5 year olds), 108 Fir Hill, 330-972-8210, **www.uakron.edu/education/community-engagement/ccd/index.dot**
Career Planning	**Career Center** (internships, cooperative education, first-job) Simmon Hall 301, 330-972-7747; **www.uakron.edu/career**

Counseling Center (group sessions, individual sessions, interactive computer program, career library) Simmons Hall 306, 330-972-7082, www.uakron.edu/counseling

Career Information (reference materials, books, etc) Bierce Library, 330-972-7234

Career Planning (two-credit course) #1100:117 emphasizes self-understanding, decision-making, and career exploration and planning.

Co-Curricular Activities

Associated Student Government, Student Union 133, 330-972-7002, www.uakron.edu/asg

Fraternities and Sororities, Office of Greek Life, Student Union 140, 330-972-7909, www.uakron.edu/studentlife/greek

Intramurals/Recreational Activities, Office of Intramural Sports, Student Recreation & Wellness Center, 330-972-7132, www.uakron.edu./srws/intramurals

Department Student Life, Student Union 211, 330-972-7866, www.uakron.edu/studentlife

SOuRCe (Student Organization Resource Center) (information on registered student organizations) Student Union 140, 330-972-7021, www.uakron.edu/studentlife/source

Zips Athletics, (schedules, events, ticket office) 330-972-6920, www.gozips.com

All Events Calendar, www.eventsatua.com

Commuter Students

Office of Off-Campus Student Services, Student Union 130, 330-972-8690, www.uakron.edu/offcampus/

Computers

Computer Based Assessment (interactive computer programs and computer based testing) Schrank Hall North 153, 330-972-6511, www.uakron.edu/it/instructional_services/cbae

Computer Solutions (sales for hardware, software, and computer accessories) Student Union Room 307, 330-972-5308, www.uakron.edu/aux/computersolutions

Zip Support Center (troubleshooting for login, e-mail, and basic computing problems) 330-972-6888, http://support.uakron.edu/wiki/index.php/Main_Page

Laptop checkout (valid Zipcard and 2nd photo ID for verification required for checkout) Bierce Library 361 and the Student Union Information Center, 2nd floor

Student Computer Support Services - SCSS (software installation, diagnostic, and repair services) Lincoln Building 103, 330-972-7626

Atomic Learning Library – From Zipline, log-on using your UANet ID and password. Click on the Student tab at the top of the screen and under "Computer Software Help!" you will see Atomic Learning. Click on Atomic Learning and explore more than 100 software learning tutorials available at your fingertips.

Disability Services	**Office of Accessibility**, Support services for students with disabilities: Learning, physical, and psychological disabilities. Simmons Hall 105, 330-972-7928, TTY/TDD: 330-972-5764, **www.uakron.edu/ access**
Education Abroad	**Office of International Programs** (Education Abroad Program - Study, Work, and Travel Abroad), Polsky 483, 330-972-6349; **www.uakron. edu/oip/**
Financial	**Office of Student Financial Aid** (grants, loans, scholarships, and work-study) Simmons Hall 202, 330-972-7032, **www.uakron.edu/ finaid**
	Office of Student Accounts (accounts receivable, cashier's office, and collections), Simmons Hall 106, 330-972-5100, **www.uakron.edu/ busfin/studentfin**
	Installment Payment Plan (allows fees to be paid on payment basis) Simmons Hall 110, 330-972-5100, **www.uakron.edu/admissions/ undergraduate/financial_aid/monthly_payment_plans.dot**
Financial Aid, Registration and Cashier's Services	**Student Services Center** (In-person assistance with financial aid, registration, and cashiers) Simmons Hall Lobby, 330-972-7272 (*information desk*), **www.uakron.edu/ssc**
Health & Wellness	**Counseling Center** (personal and confidential counseling and support services) Simmons Hall 306, 330-972-7082, **www.uakron.edu/ counseling/counseling**
	Department of Psychology Counseling Clinic (personal and career counseling conducted by graduate students) College of Arts & Science Building, Room 342, 330-972-6714, **www.uakron.edu/ psychology/academics/collaborative-program-in-counseling-psychology/dept-of-psychology-counseling-clinic.dot**
	Health Services (medical care for uncomplicated illnesses and injuries provided by registered nurses, nurse practitioners, and doctors; wellness programming) Student Recreation and Wellness Center 260, 330-972-7808, **www.uakron.edu/studentaff/health**
International Student Services	**Office of International Programs**, Polsky 483, 330-972-6349, **www.uakron.edu/oip**
Libraries	**Main Library**, Bierce Library, 330-972-8161 (reference department), **www.uakron.edu/libraries/**
	Law Library, School of Law, 330-972-7330, **www.uakron.edu/law/library/**
	Science and Technology Library, ASEC 104, 330-972-7195, **www. uakron.edu/libraries/**
	Wayne College Library, Wayne College F-Wing, 330-684-8789, **www. wayne.uakron.edu/library/**
Math Skills	**Basic Math** (course: review of arithmetic and elementary algebra) Course #2010:050 & 052

Math Lab (professional diagnosis and assistance) Bierce Library 69, 330-972-5214 and Polsky 333, 330-972-6550, **www.uakron.edu/colleges/univcoll/mathlab.php**

Medina County University Center

6300 Technology Lane, Medina OH, 44256, 330-721-2210, **www.uakron.edu/mcuc**

Mentoring

Adult Mentor Program, UA Adult Focus (adult learners assist other adult students–aged 25 years or older–transition to University life), Schrank Hall North 260, 330-972-5793, **www.uakron.edu/uaaf/mentor-program.dot**

Office of Multicultural Development (support services and peer mentoring for students of color) BCCE 115, 330-972-6769, **www.uakron.edu/multculdev**

Military Services Center

Veterans Affairs, Simmons Hall 120, 330-972-7838, **www.uakron.edu/veterans**

UA Adult Focus, Veteran Services Coordinator, 330-972-2754, **www.uakron.edu/uaaf/veterans-corner.dot**

Transfer Student Services Center (evaluation of military credit), 330-972-7009, **www.uakron.edu/transferstudents**

Parking & Shuttle Service

Parking Services (purchasing permits and parking fines) North Campus Parking Deck, 255 Buchtel Ave., 330-972-7213, **www.uakron.edu/parking/**

Roo Express Shuttle, a University owned and operated shuttle system, **www.uakron.edu/parking/roo-express/index.dot**

Personal Safety

University Police (UAPD) 146 Hill St, (non-emergencies) 330-972-7123. Dial x9911 from a campus phone for emergencies. **http://www3.uakron.edu/police/home.htm**

Campus Patrol (student members of the University Police force who can escort students around campus), 330-972-7263, **http://www3.uakron.edu/police/id92.htm**

Emergency Telephones "Blue Lights" (direct line to UAPD, more than 200 locations across campus)

Reading and Study Skills

College Reading and Study Skills (course: practice in reading comprehension skills and study techniques) Course #2010:062

Study Skills Center (professional diagnosis and assistance) Polsky 332, 330-972-6551, **www.uakron.edu/colleges/univcoll/studyskills.php**

College Survival Kit (academic performance workshops presented by Counseling Center, Simmons Hall 306, 330-972-7082, **http://www.uakron.edu/counseling/success/index.dot**

Recreation

Student Recreation & Wellness Center (rock-climbing wall, pool, work-out facilities, group exercise, intramurals, outdoor trips, weight-loss and fitness programming, massage services) 330-972-BFIT (330-972-2348), **www.uakron.edu/srws/**

Residence Life & Housing	**Department of Residence Life and Housing**, Ritchie Residence Hall 119, 330-972-7800, **www.uakron.edu/reslife**
Student Conduct	**Student Judicial Affairs** (addresses issues related to academic integrity and student rights & responsibilities) Student Union 140, 330-972-7866; **www.uakron.edu/studentlife/sja/**
Student Employment	**Office of Student Financial Aid** (functions as the personnel office for all on- campus student employees) Simmons Hall 202, 330-972-7405 **www.uakron.edu/career/student-employment/** **The Buchtelite** (university newspaper) Classified section, Student Union 51, 330-972-7919 **Career Center** (internships, cooperative education, first-job) Simmons Hall 301, 330-972-7747; **www.uakron.edu/career/**
Student Success Seminar	(two-credit course designed to identify campus resources and builds learning skills) Course #1100:101
Testing Services	**Counseling Center**, Testing services include ADHD and learning disorder assessments and many national exams such as CLEP, PRAXIS, and ACT. Simmons Hall, 304, 330-972-7084, **www.uakron.edu/counseling/testing/**
Tutorial Services	**Tutorial Center** (academic support/peer tutoring for General Education courses) Bierce Library 68, 330-972-6552, **www.uakron.edu/colleges/univcoll/tutor.php**
Wayne College	**Dean's Office**, 1901 Smucker Rd., Orrville, OH 44667, 330-684-8941, **www.wayne.uakron.edu** **Wayne College Student Services**, 330-684-8900, **http://wayne.uakron.edu/student-services/**
Writing Skills	**Basic Writing** (course: intensive practice in basic composition skills) Course #2010:042. **Writing Lab** (professional feedback and assistance) Bierce Library 69, 330-972-6548 and Polsky 303, 330-972-6984, **www.uakron.edu/colleges/univcoll/writinglab.php**
Zip Card Office & Meal Plans	**Zip Card Offices**, Student Union 106A, Simmons Hall 103 and Polsky 3rd Floor Atrium, 330-972-5637, **www.uakron.edu/aux/zipcard/** Dining plans, **www.uakron.edu/zipcard/index.dot**
Zipline	**Online Student Information Center** for registration, grades, schedules, payment, campus events, latest news, weather, etc. **www.zipline.uakron.edu**

Your Writing Process

Many people believe that a successful writer is someone who can produce an effective piece of writing in one sitting, with very little effort. But people who think this are wrong. The real truth is that writing is hard work, even for the people we call "successful writers." Successful writing is rarely produced in one sitting. Instead, it develops gradually over time as the writer moves back and forth through a process. In this material, you will learn about how you can become a successful writer by working to discover a writing process that is effective for you.

The first thing you should realize is that different writers function in different ways. Some writers cannot function without making detailed outlines, and other writers prefer to list only the main points before they draft. Some writers spend days rewriting their introductions before moving on, and others do not labor over the introduction until everything else is written. Some writers must spend most of their time thinking of ideas, and others must spend most of their time reworking their drafts. Your job is to discover writing procedures that consistently work best for you.

A first step in discovering your own successful process is to recognize that a piece of writing is usually completed over a period of time, because a writer must attend to a number of important concerns, commonly called *idea generation, drafting, revising, editing,* and *proofreading.* You should also realize that you will need to experiment with a variety of procedures for each of these aspects so you can learn which ones work well for you.

To help you experiment with developing your own successful writing process, this material describes the aspects of writing and some procedures you can try to each part of the process. As you work to develop your own successful process, keep two things in mind. First, your writing process will not move in a straight line from start to finish, from idea generation to proofreading. More likely, you will find yourself doubling back to something before going forward again. For example, while you are revising to improve your draft, you may think of a new idea to include. This means you have doubled back from the revising stage to the idea generation stage.

The second thing to remember is that the best way to improve your writing process is to pay attention to what you do when you write. Be aware of how you get ideas, write a draft, make changes, and so forth, and be aware of how satisfactory the results of these procedures are. Then make changes as you need to in order to improve your process and thus the quality of your writing. For example, if a reader tells you that you do not include enough information to prove your points, then you must improve your procedures for generating ideas and following them up. Similarly, if a reader tells you that you have too many spelling errors, you must improve the way you look for mistakes. Keep sampling techniques until you are comfortable with what you do and are satisfied with the results.

▶ IDEA GENERATION

Idea generation (discovering ideas to write about) is the earliest stage of any writing process. During idea generation, you settle on a writing topic and think about what you want to say about the topic. Because idea generation comes so early on, everything done at this stage is preliminary— all the ideas you come up with are subject to change at any time. At this point, you are more concerned with discovering what you can and will say, so you are more concerned with yourself than with your reader. Furthermore, because idea generation is preliminary, your material will be rough. That's fine because you will have plenty of time later to improve things.

Rather than wait for inspiration (which, by the way, is overrated because it seldom arrives when you need it), experienced writers go after the ideas they need. Some of the following techniques can help you do the-same.

To Discover a Writing Topic

1. Consider Your Responses to Readings in This Text Your impressions, observations, questions, points of agreement, and points of disagreement will point to one or more writing topics. For example, assume you have just read an essay about why people tell lies, and this essay makes you think that some lies are beneficial. You could, then, be prompted to write about the times when lying can be a good thing.

2. Pick a Quotation from a Reading Let your reactions to that quotation form the focus for your essay. For example, in an essay titled "Double Talk," the author says, "It was the *actions* of others, not their words, that hurt." If you feel strongly that the author is wrong because words *can* hurt us, then you could write about the ways words can hurt people.

3. Examine the Subject of a Reading from Different Angles   Answer the following questions:

A. Can I describe the subject?

B. Can I compare and/or contrast the subject with something?

C. Does the subject make me think of something else?

D. Can I explain why the subject is important or unimportant?

E. Can I agree or disagree with the author?

F. Can I relate the subject to my own experience?

G. Can I explain the causes or effects of something explained in the essay?

H. Can I give the author's ideas a larger application or relate them to something I have learned in another class?

I. What interests me about the subject?

4. Write without Stopping for Ten Minutes   Simply record any and every idea that occurs to you. Do not pause to decide whether your ideas are any good, and do not worry about grammar, spelling, or neatness. Just write without stopping, getting ideas down as they occur to you. If you run out of ideas before time is up, write the alphabet until new ideas strike you. This technique, called *freewriting,* is a way to use writing to stimulate thought. After ten minutes, read your freewriting, looking for anything— no matter how rough—that can be shaped into a writing topic. Here is an example of freewriting done after reading "Nora Quealey," a piece about the struggles of a woman trying to perform her blue-collar job in a predominantly male workplace. Notice as you read that the writer does not worry about being correct; she just gets her thoughts down the best way she can.

> Nora Quealey made me so mad I wanted to slug somebody. Here's a woman whose just trying to do her job and she has to take all this crud from guys on some kind of a power trip. Sexual harassment is so real and people don't even realize it. I was always taking stuff from guys when I worked as a waitress and I could never say anything because the customer is always right.
>
> These guys would come on to me and pat me and I'd have to smile and make excuses to leave. What else? Let's see? What can I say. Well I guess some girls do ask for it because they dress sexy, like they want guys to notice and that makes it hard for everyone else. Do they deserve it? Maybe so but I'm not sure. I guess so. Tough question I guess most guys would say yes. Some women don't think its' harrassment. That really fries me. I'm tired I worked last night. Is this enough stuff. Oh yeah, I work on campus now and policies are on the bulatin board about sexual harrassment so I haven't had any trouble at all in the cafeteria where I work.

The student's freewriting suggests several topics to write about:

A. Why some people don't take sexual harassment seriously.

B. The author's experiences with sexual harassment when she was a waitress.

c. Whether women who dress in a sexy manner deserve sexual harassment.

D. How places of employment can prevent sexual harassment.

5. Try Mapping   To map, write the name of a broad subject area in a circle in the center of a piece of paper, like this:

Then think of ideas related to that subject and add them, like this:

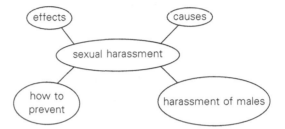

Continue thinking of related ideas and joining them to the appropriate circles until you get something like this:

The previous mapping gives you four possible topics: causes of sexual harassment, effects of sexual harassment, how to prevent sexual harassment, and harassment of males. For three of these topics, mapping brings out some ideas that can be included in the writing.

To Discover Ideas for Writing about a Topic

1. Write a Discovery Draft   This is not really a first draft; it is a form of preliminary writing to help you determine what you know and don't know about a topic. To write a discovery draft, spill out everything you can think of on your topic. Don't agonize over anything; just get things down the best way you can. When you can think of nothing else, go over the draft to decide which ideas are suitable for your next draft—this one will really be your "first" draft. If you cannot think of much to say in your discovery draft, you may not know enough about your topic, and you should consider changing it or trying other idea generation techniques.

2. List Every Idea You Can Think of Related to Your Topic   Do not pause to evaluate whether you have good ideas or not—just write whatever occurs to you. When you can think of nothing else, go over your list to decide which ideas to include in your first draft. If you want, you can number the ideas in the order you want to handle them in your draft, and this will give you a scratch outline. Here is a sample listing for an essay about the causes of sexual harassment. Notice that all ideas were listed and ones that did not prove usable were crossed out.

> men don't respect women
>
> women don't stand up for themselves
>
> employers don't take it seriously
>
> men are taught that women are sex objects
>
> some women encourage harassment
>
> ~~men are harassed too~~
>
> companies don't have policies
>
> ~~women are victims~~

3. Answer Questions about Your Topic   You may get ideas for writing about your topic by answering questions like these:

A. What is the most important point I want to make?
B. Why is this point important?
C. Why is this point true?
D. What examples prove this point or illustrate it?
E. To whom does this point matter? Why?
F. What is my attitude about this topic?

In addition, you can get ideas by answering the standard journalist's questions: Who? What? When? Where? Why? How?

4. Try Mapping   Previously you learned about mapping to discover a topic. Mapping can also help you come up with ideas once you have that topic. In the center of the page, write your topic with a circle around it. Then as ideas occur to you, join them to the appropriate circles. In addition to helping you think of ideas, mapping has the advantage of showing how your ideas related to each other. Here is an example of a mapping to discover ideas to develop the topic "how to prevent sexual harassment."

5. Talk to Other People about Your Topic   They may have suggestions for you. In particular, the students in your writing class may have ideas you can include in your writing. Also, if your campus has a writing center, the tutors there can work collaboratively with you to help you come up with ideas.

▶ DRAFTING

Drafting is a first effort at getting your ideas down in essay form. First drafts are almost always rough, so do not worry if yours seems to need a great deal of work. A draft is only meant to produce raw material that can be gradually shaped during the revision process that comes later. Writers often find that drafting goes more smoothly if they write an outline first. Some writers favor a detailed outline with roman numerals, letters, and numbers; other writers prefer a scratch outline that lists only the main points they will cover and the order they will cover them in. Experiment with both kinds of outlines to discover which one works better for you. (Some writers even like to outline a draft *after* it is written to check organization and development.) In addition, some of the following tips should help you when you draft:

1. *Let your draft be rough.* If you expect this early attempt to be polished, you will become frustrated. Remember, you will have plenty of opportunity to improve things later when you revise.
2. *Skip troublesome parts.* Concentrate on what you *can* do and leave the rest for later. If you stop to wrestle with each problem along the way, you may become discouraged. So if you cannot think of a word, leave a blank; check spellings later; leave space to add support if you are not sure how to back up a point. Just keep pushing forward.

3. *If you cannot get anything down on paper, return to idea generation.* Perhaps you thought you were ready to draft, but you did not have enough ideas after all. That is okay. Just go back now and generate more ideas. Writers often move back and forth through the writing process.

4. *If you have trouble expressing yourself in writing, try writing the way you speak.* Speaking may come more naturally to you than writing. You can always revise later to make your prose more formal, if necessary. As an alternative, speak your "draft" into a tape recorder and then transcribe the tape. Again, you can revise later to meet the conventions of written English.

5. *Write as fast as you can.* You may be more successful getting a draft down if you race through from start to finish, not allowing yourself to stop if you get stuck or when you know something must be revised. Remember, you are now seeking only raw material that you can shape later, when you revise.

▶ REVISING

Once your draft is down, no matter how rough it is, you have raw material to shape into a form suitable to show a reader. When you shape a draft to prepare it for a reader, you are *revising*. To revise, focus on content, organization, and expressing yourself effectively. Save grammar, spelling, and punctuation for later, when you edit. Remember that revising is more than just changing a word or two; it is a thoroughgoing rethinking and reworking of the draft. Some of the following tips may help you when you revise.

1. Leave Your Work before You Revise   Try to pace your writing so that you have time to leave your work for a day or so after drafting and before revising. This way, your draft can "cool," and you will stand a better chance of finding problems. Of course, if you are going to follow this suggestion, you cannot put off your writing until the last minute.

2. Make the Easy Changes First   Build momentum as you come into the more difficult changes. Success breeds success, so after successfully completing easier revisions, you may find harder ones less challenging.

3. Read Your Draft Aloud to Listen for Problems   Sometimes you *hear* difficulties that you fail to *see*. One word of caution is in order here: you will have a tendency to read what you *meant* to write rather than what you actually *did* write, so be careful to read exactly what is on the page.

4. If You Wrote Your Draft by Hand, Type a Fresh Copy before Revising You may be more likely to notice problems in type than in your own handwriting.

5. Ask Two or Three Reliable Readers to Look at Your Draft They can suggest changes. Be sure that your readers are capable of judging your work responsibly and that they won't hesitate to offer constructive criticism. (If friends or family members cannot be objective or critical, they are not helpful readers.) Weigh your readers' responses carefully; you have the final say about what to revise. (If your school has a writing center, you can find reliable readers there.)

6. Revise in Stages and over a Period of Days Revising is time-consuming and tiring, so be prepared to leave your work whenever you need a break. Also, be prepared to spend several days revising; this is a task that cannot be hurried.

7. Use a Checklist You will remember what you need to consider. Here is one you may find convenient:

A. Be sure your writing has an unmistakable thesis. (A *thesis* is the controlling idea of the writing; this is the point that everything else in the writing relates to.)
B. Be sure all your points are related to your thesis. Check every sentence to be sure that it is clearly and directly relevant. If something does not relate to the thesis, then it should be eliminated or reworked to be made relevant.
C. Be sure that every point you make is backed up with evidence and/or explanation and/or examples.
D. Be sure your points are in a logical order.
E. Be sure your introduction creates interest.
F. Be sure your conclusion ties things up.
G. Be sure all your points are clear.
H. Eliminate unnecessary words. For example, change "Her hair was red in color" to "Her hair was red."
I. Substitute specific words for vague ones. For example, instead of saying "The dog chased the ball," say "The black labrador chased the tennis ball."

8. Do Not Edit Stick to the revision concerns (content, organization, and effective expression) and avoid dealing with grammar, punctuation, and spelling. Editing too early will distract you from the larger revision issues. Furthermore, it is inefficient to worry about editing details—say, the spelling of a word—since you may eliminate the word as you revise.

9. Trust Your Instincts If you sense something is wrong, assume the feeling is correct and revise the portion in question. Even if you cannot name it, the problem probably exists.

When you are satisfied with your changes to improve content, organization, and expression, you can move on to matters of grammatical correctness, spelling, punctuation, and capitalization. This is *editing,* and you must not skip it, because readers rapidly grow annoyed by writing with many errors in it. Of course, during editing, ideas may occur to you for revising, and you should respond to them; writers often step back before going forward.

Some of the following tips may help you edit:

1. *Leave your work for a day* to clear your head and increase your chances of finding mistakes.
2. *Edit more than once.* The first time through, look for any kind of mistake. After that, look for the kinds of mistakes you are in the habit of making.
3. *Place a ruler under each line and point to each word and punctuation mark as you go.* This procedure helps you move slowly enough to notice errors. Otherwise, you may go too quickly and overlook mistakes.
4. *Read your writing backward, from last sentence to first sentence.* This procedure can force you to see what is on the page, rather than what you mean to write.
5. *Learn the rules.* You cannot be a confident editor without knowing the grammar and usage rules, so each time your instructor or another reader calls an error to your attention, take the time to look up and learn the appropriate rule.
6. *Trust your instincts.* If something sounds "off," a problem probably exists.
7. *Get help.* You can ask a reliable reader, perhaps from your campus writing center, to help you edit. But remember, the responsibility to learn and apply the rules is yours, so use a reliable reader only as backup support.

▶ PROOFREADING

After editing, prepare a clean typed, computer-generated, or neatly written copy of your work for your reader. Before submitting your writing, however, be sure to check for typing or copying errors. If you find a mistake, make the correction neatly on the page. Of course, if you must make many corrections, rewrite or retype the page.

Proofreading must be done slowly to be effective. (The preceding tips for editing also apply to proofreading.)

The following pages show how Erika, a student writer, worked through idea generation, drafting, revising, and editing for an assignment calling for an essay about an issue in the news. For her essay she chose to argue against raising the minimum wage.

Examining Erika's material will give you a sense of how the writing process can work.

Erika's List

To generate ideas, Erika wrote a list, which produced enough material to get her started. You may need to use a different idea generation technique, or you may need to use a combination of techniques. Remember, each writer must find his or her own best procedures.

List

Notice that Erika used abbreviations. She wrote whatever occurred to her and did not censor herself.

Most people think raising the min. wage is a good idea.

It creates more problems than it solves.

Min. wage earners = not usually breadwinners, but teens (econ class)

Teens will lose their jobs because expenses will go up for employers.

Ideas she decided not to include were crossed out. She also noted in parentheses what she learned in economics class.

~~People who favor raising min. wage are uneducated.~~

Unskilled workers make min. wage & we have shortage of unskilled workers (econ. class)

~~Unskilled workers don't deserve more money.~~

Not an incentive to get off welfare.

Erika's First Draft

Erika felt her list yielded enough material for a first draft. She wrote her draft without the benefit of an outline. However, you may find that your draft goes more smoothly if you develop an outline to serve as a guide to drafting.

First Draft

A proposal to raise the minimum wage is in the news again. Every time we turn around Congress is proposing bills for an increase in the minimum wage. Republicans are stereotyped as the opposition and the Democrats are stereotyped as the supporters, but do we really need a higher minimum wage? No, a higher minimum wage wouldn't help the majority of the people earning minimum wage. It would do more harm to these people than it would help.

Many people who support a raise in the minimum wage do not understand that it will have a negative effect on national unemployment, inflation, and employment opportunities for the unskilled.

The most common misunderstanding is that the average minimum wage earner is the breadwinner supporting the family. Actually, the minimum wage earner is usually a teenager or a second family income, as I learned in my economics class.

If we raise the minimum wage, these teenagers will lose their jobs because employers will think it costs too much to keep them on, which will increase the unemployment rate among teens, which will lead to all kinds of social problems.

Another common misunderstanding is that raising the minimum wage will help the welfare system. Some people think that a higher minimum wage will encourage people to get off welfare and look for a job. While some people might be encouraged to look for work, the unskilled jobs many of them need will no longer exist because they were eliminated to save costs that resulted from the higher minimum wage. New entry-level jobs will not be created because they will be to costly. Thus, the rolls of welfare will not be reduced at all.

Raising the minimum wage does appear on the surface to be a good idea, but it will do more harm than good.

Reader Response to Erika's First Draft

To get suggestions before revising, Erika asked a classmate to answer the questions in the following Reader Response Form. Before you revise, you can also use the questions on this form to get responses to your draft.

Reader Response Form

1. What is the thesis idea?
   Raising the minimum wage is not a good idea.
2. Is there anything unrelated to the thesis idea?
   Everything seems related to the thesis idea.
3. Are any points unproven or unexplained?
   It seems like you have excellent ideas to defend your view, but you never really explain them. For example, in paragraph 2 you mention inflation, but you never discuss it. You also say that if teenagers lose their jobs, then there will be social problems as a result. What problems? I think almost everything you say needs more explanation.
4. Is anything unclear?
   I don't really understand how minimum wage jobs can be eliminated. How will the work get done then?
5. Are the ideas in a logical order?
   yes
6. Does the opening create interest?
   The opening isn't bad, but it's not very exciting either. Should the first two paragraphs be joined?
7. Does the conclusion bring the piece to a satisfying finish?
   The ending just repeats the thesis. It seems lazy.
8. What do you like best about the essay?
   I think the way the welfare point is developed is strong because it has some detail to it. I also think the points are well thought out. They just need to be explained more. I think I could learn something from this essay.

Erika's Second List

After studying her classmate's response to her draft, Erika decided she needed more ideas, so she did additional listing to focus on developing the points in her draft.

Social Problems That Result When Teenagers Lose Their Jobs

time on their hands leads to getting into trouble

teens turn to crime to get money

teens turn to drugs

teens spend time on the streets

won't get the experience and training needed to move on to better jobs

Unemployment

entry-level jobs for the unskilled will be lost

ranks of the unemployed will grow

ranks of welfare recipients will grow

Erika's Revision

When Erika revised, she considered her reader's response and her additional idea generation material. She did not limit herself to the points her reader made, though. She also made other changes she thought would strengthen the piece.

Revision

Comments:
Erika reworked her introduction. It is shorter, with a clear thesis. Paragraph 2, which seemed like a thesis, is eliminated.

In response to her reader's criticism, Erika developed her point about social problems more.

Erika adds the point that unemployment will increase.

A proposal to raise the minimum wage is in the news again. Every time we turn around Congress is proposing bills for an increase in the minimum wage. However, raising the minimum wage is not a good idea because it will create a number of serious problems.

Many people think that the minimum wage earner is a breadwinner supporting a family. However, I learned in my economics class that usually the minimum wage earner is a teenager. If we raise the minimum wage, these teenagers will lose their jobs because employers will think it costs too much to keep them on. Then, unemployment will increase among teens, which will lead to all kinds of social problems. Without jobs, teenagers will have too much time on their hands, so they may begin hanging out on the streets, where they may take up drug use. Without jobs, teenagers will also lose a source of income. To get money, some will turn to crime. Also, teens will lose the opportunity to gain work experience and training which can help them move on to better jobs.

Raising the minimum wage will lead to the loss of jobs. Because employers will not be able to pay the extra salaries, they will have to eliminate minimum wage jobs. Since minimum wage jobs are usually unskilled jobs, many unskilled workers will be unable to find work. This will cause the ranks of the unemployed to grow.

With increased unemployment will come an increase in welfare recipients. Some people think that a higher minimum wage will encourage people to get off welfare and look for a job. While some people might be encouraged to look for work, the unskilled jobs many of them need will no longer exist because they were eliminated to save costs that resulted from the higher minimum wage. Thus, the rolls of welfare will not be reduced at all.

Raising the minimum wage may seem like a good idea on the surface, but it will do more harm than good.

Teacher Response to Erika's Revision

Erika,

You have an important topic here, and you seem to have given it careful consideration. In fact, a topic this important deserves the strongest possible introduction. Think about reworking yours to be sure you capture your reader's interest. Paragraph 2 is your strongest paragraph because it is well developed and clear. I'm wondering, though, why loss of teenage jobs is such a problem. Can't teens be guided away from the streets, drug, and crime if they don't work? Can you revise paragraph 3 to make it stronger? Part of that paragraph seems to repeat paragraph 2. Your transition from the discussion of unemployment to welfare is very smooth, but your conclusion needs attention. It seems abrupt. I'm wondering if you can conclude effectively by discussing alternatives to raising the minimum wage.

Erika's Idea Generation

After reading her instructor's comments, Erika decided to try some additional idea generation to develop ideas on alternatives to raising the minimum wage. This time, she tried mapping. Here are the results:

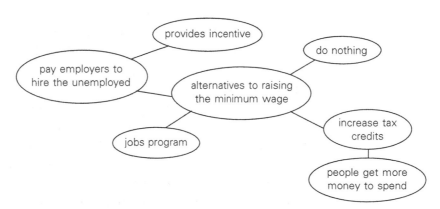

Erika's Final Draft

Erika revised her essay through two more drafts and then carefully edited. The final version appears here.

Comments:

Erika added a title.

The introduction was revised to create reader interest. The thesis remains the same.

Because her teacher considered paragraph 2 to be strong, Erika left this paragraph as it was.

In response to her teacher's question, Erika offers more on why loss of teen jobs is a problem.

At her teacher's suggestion, Erika eliminated repetition from this paragraph and strengthened the detail.

At her teacher's suggestion, Erika improved her conclusion by discussing alternatives to raising the minimum wage.

Raising the minimum wage: trouble on the horizon

So you think raising the minimum wage is a good idea, do you? Why not? Everyone else does, including many members of Congress who seem to be proposing bills to increase the wage more often than some people brush their teeth. However, despite public and Congressional support, raising the minimum wage is not a good idea because it will create a number of serious problems.

Many people think that the minimum wage earner is a breadwinner supporting a family. However, I learned in my economics class that usually the minimum wage earner is a teenager. If we raise the minimum wage, these teenagers will lose their jobs because employers will think it costs too much to keep them on. Then, unemployment will increase among teens, which will lead to all kinds of social problems. Without jobs, teenagers will have too much time on their hands, so they may begin hanging out on the streets, where they may take up drug use. Without jobs, teenagers will also lose a source of income. To get money, some will turn to crime. Also, teens will lose the opportunity to gain work experience and training which can help them move on to better jobs.

Some people may think that it is not a big problem if teenagers lose their jobs. They can be guided into other areas to keep them off the streets and away from drugs and crime. However, the money teens make is not always extra income that goes for clothes, CDs, and the hot new tennis shoes. Many families depend on this extra income to make ends meet. Other families expect this money to finance college. Thus, if teenagers lose their minimum wage jobs, some families will face a hardship, and some teenagers will have to give up dreams of college.

Teenagers will not be the only ones who lose jobs if the minimum wage is increased. Many unskilled workers hold minimum wage jobs, and they will be affected. Once the jobs held by unskilled workers become too expensive for employers, these jobs will be consolidated or eliminated wherever possible, putting more people in the unemployment lines.

With increased unemployment will come an increase in welfare recipients. Some people think that raising the minimum wage will encourage people to get off welfare and look for a job. While some people might be encouraged to look for work, the unskilled jobs many of them need will no longer exist because they were eliminated to save costs that resulted from the higher minimum wage. Thus, the rolls of welfare will not be reduced at all.

Although raising the minimum wage is not a good idea, people who want to do so have some good reasons. They hope to increase the amount of money people have, and they hope to reduce welfare rolls. However, these worthy goals can be achieved in other ways. For example, the government can offer tax credits to those who earn minimum wage.

This will give minimum wage earners more money without creating the problems associated with raising the minimum wage. The government could also use job training programs to train those on welfare for jobs that would keep them employed. In addition, the government could pay employers a stipend or offer them a tax break if they hire people who are currently unemployed. Any of these plans would increase the income of people who need the money and help reduce the welfare and unemployment rolls. Thus, raising the minimum wage, which would create problems, is not the best course of action.

Freewriting

Peter Elbow

▶ **PREREADING: BACKGROUND**

Peter Elbow, an English professor at the University of Massachusetts at Amherst, was born in New York City and was educated at Williams College, Exeter College at Oxford, and Brandeis University. He has written *Writing without Teachers* and *Writing with Power,* two well-known books about the writing process.

In the following essay, Elbow explains how writers can use freewriting to discover new ideas as well as their own voices, their "only source of power." He also stresses the idea that "premature editing" will lead only to dull, lifeless prose. Ideas such as these have helped students and teachers alike to rethink the writing process and become strong, effective writers.

▶ **PREREADING: QUESTIONS**

1. Describe your own writing process. What do you do when you have to write something?
2. What did you learn about the writing process in high school or in some other English class?
3. How important is editing (the act of making sure that words are spelled correctly, sentences are grammatical, punctuation has been used properly, and so forth)?

▶ **HELPFUL DEFINITIONS**

coherent (3)—logically ordered
interposes (4)—interjects
inhibited (6)—restrained
tactic (8)—plan
vacuums (10)—empty spaces

Freewriting

Peter Elbow

1   The most effective way I know to improve your writing is do freewriting exercises regularly. At least three times a week. They are sometimes called "automatic writing," "babbling," or "jabbering" exercises. The idea is simply to write for ten minutes (later on, perhaps fifteen or twenty). Don't stop for anything. Go quickly without rushing. Never stop to look back, to cross something out, to wonder how to spell something, to wonder what word or thought to use, or to think about what you are doing. If you can't think of a word or spelling, just use a squiggle or else write, "I can't think of it." Just put down something. The easiest thing is just to put down whatever is in your mind. If you get stuck it's fine to write "I can't think what to say, I can't think what to say" as many times as you want, or repeat the last word you wrote over and over again; or anything else. The only requirement is that you *never* stop.

2   What happens to a freewriting exercise is important. It must be a piece of writing which, even if someone reads it, doesn't send any ripples back to you. It is like writing something and putting it in a bottle in the sea. The teacherless class helps your writing by providing maximum feedback. Freewritings help you by providing no feedback at all. When I assign one, I invite the writer to let me read it. But also tell him to keep it if he prefers. I read it quickly and make no comments at all and I do not speak with him about it. The main thing is that a freewriting must never be evaluated in any way; in fact there must be no discussion or comment at all.

3   Here is an example of a fairly coherent exercise (sometimes they are very incoherent, which is fine):

4   I think I'll write what's on my mind, but the only thing on my mind right now is what to write for ten minutes. I've never done this before and I'm not prepared in any way—the sky is cloudy today, how's that? now I'm afraid I won't be able to think of what to write when I get to the end of the sentence—well, here I am at the end of the sentence—here I am again, again, again, again, at least I'm still writing—Now I ask is there some reason to be happy that I'm still writing—ah yes! Here comes the question again—What am I getting out of this? What point is there in it? It's almost obscene to always ask it but I seem to question everything that way and I was gonna say something else pertaining to that but I got so busy writing down the first part that I forgot what I was leading into. This is kind of fun oh don't stop writing—cars and trucks speeding by somewhere out the window, pens clittering across people's papers. The sky is cloudy—is it symbolic that I should be mentioning it? Huh? I dunno. Maybe I should try colors, blue, red, dirty words—wait a minute—no can't do that, orange, yellow, arm tired, green pink violet magenta lavender red brown black green—now that I can't think of any more colors—just about done—relief? maybe.

Freewriting may seem crazy but actually it makes simple sense. Think of the difference between speaking and writing. Writing has the advantage of permitting more editing. But that's its downfall too. Almost everybody interposes a massive and complicated series of editings between the time words start to be born into consciousness and when they finally come off the end of the pencil or typewriter onto the page. This is partly because schooling makes us obsessed with the "mistakes" we make in writing. Many people are constantly thinking about spelling and grammar as they try to write. I am always thinking about the awkwardness, wordiness, and general mushiness of my natural verbal product as I try to write down words.

5   But it's not just "mistakes" or "bad writing" we edit as we write. We also edit unacceptable thoughts and feelings, as we do in speaking. In writing there is more time to do it so the editing is heavier: when speaking, there's someone right there waiting for a reply and he'll get bored or think we're crazy if we don't come out with *something*. Most of the time in speaking, we settle for the catch-as-catch-can way in which the words tumble out. In writing, however, there's a chance to try to get them right. But the opportunity to get them right is a terrible burden: you can work for two hours trying to get a paragraph "right" and discover it's not right at all. And then give up.

6   Editing, *in itself,* is not the problem. Editing is usually necessary if we want to end up with something satisfactory. The problem is that editing goes on *at the same time* as producing. The editor is, as it were, constantly looking over the shoulder of the producer and constantly fiddling with what he's doing while he's in the middle of trying to do it. No wonder the producer gets nervous, jumpy, inhibited, and finally can't be coherent. It's an unnecessary burden to try to think of words and also worry at the same time whether they're the right words.

7   The main thing about freewriting is that it is *nonediting.* It is an exercise in bringing together the process of producing words and putting them down on the page. Practiced regularly, it undoes the ingrained habit of editing at the same time you are trying to produce. It will make writing less blocked because words will come more easily. You will use up more paper, but chew up fewer pencils.

8   Next time you write, notice how often you stop yourself from writing down something you were going to write down. Or else cross it out after it's written. "Naturally," you say, "it wasn't any good." But think for a moment about the occasions when you spoke well. Seldom was it because you first got the beginning just right. Usually it was a matter of a halting or even garbled beginning, but you kept going and your speech finally become coherent and even powerful. There is a lesson here for writing: trying to get the beginning just right is a formula for failure—and probably a secret tactic to make yourself give up writing. Make some words, whatever they are, and then grab hold of that line and reel in as hard

as you can. Afterwards you can throw away lousy beginnings and make new ones. This is the quickest way to get into good writing.

9   The habit of compulsive, premature editing doesn't just make writing hard. It also makes writing dead. Your voice is damped out by all the interruptions, changes, and hesitations between the consciousness and the page. In your natural way of producing words there is a sound, a texture, a rhythm—a voice—which is the main source of power in your writing. I don't know how it works, but this voice is the force that will make a reader listen to you, the energy that drives the meanings through his thick skull. Maybe you don't *like* your voice; maybe people have made fun of it. But it's the only voice you've got. It's your only source of power. You better get back into it, no matter what you think of it. If you keep writing in it, it may change into something you like better. But if you abandon it, you'll likely never have a voice and never be heard.

10   Freewritings are vacuums. Gradually you will begin to carry over into your regular writing some of the voice, force, and connectedness that creep into those vacuums.

▲

▶ QUESTIONS ON CONTENT

1. What is freewriting?
2. Elbow insists that "freewriting may seem crazy but actually it makes simple sense" (paragraph 4). Examine the sample passage of freewriting included in the essay, and then agree or disagree with Elbow's statement. Explain your answer.
3. What distinction does Elbow make between speaking and writing?
4. What problems can editing cause a writer? How can editing help a writer?
5. Elbow devotes paragraph 9 to the discussion of voice (the way the writer sounds). Explain why he considers voice so important.

▶ QUESTIONS ON TECHNIQUE

1. Which sentence presents the thesis (main idea) of the essay?
2. Why do you think Elbow includes such an extensive example of freewriting?
3. In paragraph 2, Elbow explains why learning the process of freewriting is important. Why does he include this information? Why does he place it in such an early paragraph?
4. At the end of the essay, Elbow explains the importance of voice (the way a writer sounds). A writer's voice can be serious, casual, playful, angry, formal, sarcastic, and so forth. Describe Elbow's voice in the essay. What kind of person do you imagine him to be? Why do you think Elbow uses the voice that he does?

Freewrite on a topic of your choice. (If you cannot decide on a topic, write about how you feel about writing.) Then examine what you have written. Which of your ideas do you find the most interesting? Will you use freewriting in the future? Why or why not?

► COLLABORATIVE ACTIVITY

A writer does not always use the same voice. For example, when writing to a future employer, you may try to sound formal and polite. However, when you write to a close friend, you will sound casual and informal. In a group, experiment with your own voices. Think about a problem on your campus. First write a short letter explaining the problem to a friend who attends a different school, and then write a short letter explaining the same problem to the president or dean of your institution. Compare the two letters, noting the differences.

► WRITING TOPICS

1. Elbow makes the distinction between writing and speaking. Based on your own experience, write an essay explaining whether you prefer to speak or write. Also explain the reason(s) for your preferences.

2. Do you remember a time when you wrote something that made you proud? Describe the piece of writing and the process you followed to complete it.

3. Elbow, a writing expert, explains the process of freewriting. Like Elbow, think about something you do well (plant a garden, throw a curve ball, plan a party, etc.), and then write an essay explaining how to do it.

4. What is your definition of good writing? Use examples from your own writing and/or someone else's to illustrate ideas.

5. Write a humorous definition of bad writing.

Revising

Writers usually produce drafts that require a substantial amount of reworking. Most often, you will need to study your draft carefully and objectively to discover ways to improve the content, organization, and expression of ideas. This kind of reworking is revising, *and it is hard work.*

"I Don't Like My Draft."

You've just placed the final period at the end of the last sentence of your first draft, and you're feeling pretty proud of yourself. So you lean back, put your feet up on the desk, and start to reread the masterpiece. But as you read, you start to feel less and less proud—your masterpiece isn't nearly as good as you thought it was. Does this mean you have to start over? Probably not. Instead, try some of the suggestions in this chapter.

► BE REALISTIC

Remember that another name for a first draft is a *rough* draft. The first attempt is supposed to have problems—even lots of them. So do not build in frustration by expecting too much of yourself too soon. Instead, realize that your first pass is bound to be rough, roll up your sleeves, and get in there and revise until you are happy with the results.

► WALK AWAY

Before deciding about the quality of your draft, leave it for a while so you can clear your head and regain your objectivity. The longer you can stay away, the better; but walk away for at least several hours—for a day if you have the time. When you return to your draft and reread it, you may discover potential that you overlooked previously.

▶ SHARE THE DRAFT

Sometimes writers tend to be too hard on themselves, especially in the early drafting stage. Instead of recognizing the potential in their drafts, they see only the rough spots. As a result, they become frustrated and start over when it's not really necessary. Before deciding about the quality of your draft, share it with several people whose judgment you trust. Ask these readers to note all the strengths in the draft and all the areas that can be made strong with some polishing. When you review your readers' comments, you may realize how much potential your draft has.

▶ LISTEN TO YOUR DRAFT

Your draft may seem worse than it is if it is messy or written in a sloppy handwriting or written in pencil or written on paper ripped out of a spiral notebook. In short, the overall appearance of the draft may affect your evaluation of it. To judge the worth of your draft more reliably, ask someone to read it to you. As you listen, you may discover sections that are far stronger than you realized.

▶ TRY TO SALVAGE SOMETHING

If you are convinced that your draft is awful and that you must begin again, at least try to salvage something. Perhaps you can use the same approach to your introduction, or some of your examples, or several of your main ideas. While it is tempting to rip the draft to shreds and begin anew, you may not have to begin again at square 1. If you look closely at your draft, some of your work may be usable in your new draft.

▶ WRITE A SECOND DRAFT WITHOUT LOOKING AT THE FIRST

Try writing a second version without looking at the first. This technique is often successful because you manage to retain the best parts of the first draft, eliminate the weakest parts, and add some new, effective material. The key to this technique is to avoid referring to the first draft while writing the second.

▶ DON'T DESPAIR IF YOU MUST START OVER

Writers start over all the time because often we must discover what we do *not* want to do before we discover what we *do* want to do; sometimes we must learn what we can *not* do before we are clear about what we *can* do. So if you must begin again, do not be discouraged; keep your attitude positive. After all, your earlier draft or drafts were not a waste of your time— they were groundwork, preliminary efforts that paved the way for your most recent effort.

▶ DO THE BEST YOU CAN WITH WHAT
  YOU HAVE

Yes, writers start over all the time, but writers do not usually have an unlimited amount of time to work within. At some point you must force yourself to push forward, even if you are not completely comfortable with the status of your first draft. Not every piece can be a shining moment, so when time is running out, do the best you can with what you have and be satisfied that you have met your deadline.

"I Don't Know What to Change."

Good news! You finished your first draft, and now you are ready to dig in and make all those changes that will improve your writing and make it fit for a reader. So you read your draft—but wait a minute—everything seems fine. *You* understand what you mean; everything seems clear and well developed to *you*. In fact, you can't figure out what changes to make. Well, the truth is that as the writer, you may have no trouble at all figuring out what you meant when you wrote all those words, but that does not guarantee that the reader will have as easy a time of it. In order to revise successfully, you must view your draft as the reader will and make changes to meet your reader's needs. The suggestions in this chapter can help.

▶ WALK AWAY

Before revising, the smartest thing you can do is leave your work for a day, even longer if you can manage it. Getting away from your writing gives you a chance to clear your head and regain your objectivity so that when you return to revise, you stand a better chance of seeing your work the way your reader will.

▶ TYPE YOUR DRAFT

After writing your draft, type it into a neat copy and then read it over. Problems that you overlook in your own handwriting may be more apparent in typed form because the copy resembles printed material rather than your own handiwork. As a result, it can be easier to be objective about the writing.

Also, some mistakes may leap out at you. For example, a paragraph that ran the better part of a page in your handwritten copy may be only three lines in typed form—a visual signal that more detail may be needed.

▶ LISTEN TO YOUR DRAFT

Many times we can hear problems that we overlook visually. For this reason, writers should read their drafts out loud at least once. When you read aloud, be sure to go slowly and be careful to read exactly what is on the page. If you read quickly, you are likely to read what you *meant* to write rather than what you actually *did* write.

Some writers do well if they read their drafts into a tape recorder. Then they play back the tape to listen for problems.

Still other writers prefer to have other people read their drafts to them. Sometimes, another person's tone of voice helps the writer pick up on problems.

▶ UNDERLINE MAIN POINTS

A good way to determine if you have supported your points is to go through your draft and underline every main point. Then go back and check to see what appears after each underlined point. If one underlined point is immediately followed by another underlined point, you have not supported a main idea. Similarly, if an underlined idea is followed by only one or two sentences, you should consider whether you have enough support.

▶ OUTLINE YOUR DRAFT AFTER WRITING IT

A good way to determine if your ideas follow logically one to the next is to outline your draft *after* writing it. If you have points that do not fit into the outline at the appropriate spots, you have discovered an organization problem.

▶ REVISE IN STAGES

When you revise, you have a great deal to consider—so much, in fact, that you may overlook some things. One way to avoid overlooking important considerations is to revise in stages, following one of these patterns:

▷ **Easy to hard** First make all the easy changes, take a break, and then go on to make the more difficult changes. Take a break whenever you become tired or when you get stuck. Making the easy changes first may help you build enough momentum to carry you through the harder changes.

▷ **Hard to easy** First make some of your more difficult changes, take a break, make some more of your difficult changes, take another break, and continue with the harder changes, taking breaks as needed. When you have finished the more difficult changes, take a break and tackle the easier changes. Some writers like the psychological high that comes from getting the hard changes out of the way and knowing the rest of revision is downhill.

▷ **Paragraph by paragraph** Revise your first paragraph until it is as perfect as you can make it, and then go to the next paragraph. Proceed paragraph by paragraph, taking a break after every paragraph or two.

▷ **Content–organization–effective expression** First make all your content changes: for adequate detail, relevant detail, specific detail, clarity, and suitable introduction and conclusion. Then take a break and check the organization: logical order of ideas, effective thesis, and clear topic sentences. Take another break and revise for sentence effectiveness: effective word choice, smooth flow, helpful transitions.

▶ SHARE YOUR INTRODUCTION
   AND CONCLUSION

To help you judge the effectiveness of your introduction and conclusion, type up these parts of your writing separately, and give them to two or three people to read. Ask them whether they would be interested in reading something that opened and closed with these paragraphs.

▶ SHARE YOUR DRAFT WITH A
   RELIABLE READER

If you have trouble deciding what changes to make, ask someone to react to your draft and suggest revisions. To get the most constructive criticism possible, be sure your reader is reliable. That is, be sure your reader is someone who knows about the qualities of effective writing. Also, be sure your reader will not hesitate to offer criticism. If your roommate is afraid of hurting your feelings, do not ask that person to read your draft. Similarly, if your cousin has failed a writing course twice, don't ask your cousin to react to your draft.

If your school has a writing center, stop in to get a reliable reaction to your draft. Typically, writing center staff members are trained to provide sensitive responses to student writing.

A good way to identify changes that should be made in your draft is to consider your detail in light of your reader's point of view. Different readers will place different demands on a writer. For example, assume you are writing to convince your reader to vote for a school levy that will increase property taxes. If your audience is someone with children in the school system, explaining that the additional revenue will go toward enhancing the art and music curriculum may be sufficiently persuasive. However, if your reader is a childless retired person on a fixed income, this argument may not be very convincing. Instead, you may need to explain that better schools will cause the reader's home to increase in value so the resale price is high.

To evaluate your detail in terms of your reader's point of view, construct a reader profile by answering the following ten questions:

1. How much education does my reader have?
2. What is my reader's age, sex, race, nationality, and religion?
3. What is my reader's occupation and socioeconomic level?
4. What part of the country does my reader live in? Does my reader live in an urban or rural area?
5. What is my reader's political affiliation?
6. How familiar is my reader with my topic?
7. What does my reader need to know to appreciate my point of view?
8. How resistant will my reader be to my point of view?
9. How hard will I have to work to create interest in my topic?
10. Does my reader have any special hobbies or interests or concerns that will affect how my essay is viewed? Is my reader chiefly concerned with money? career? the environment? society? religion? family?

After answering these questions, review your draft with an eye toward providing detail suited to your reader's unique makeup.

▶ PRETEND TO BE SOMEONE ELSE

To be more objective about your work so you can decide what to change, pretend you are someone else. Read your draft as the judge of a contest who will award you $10,000 for a prize-winning essay. Or become the editor of a magazine who is deciding what changes to make in the draft before publishing the piece. Or read as your worst enemy, someone who loves to find fault with your work. Assuming a new personality as you read your draft may help you depersonalize your work enough to allow you to find what should be revised.

To be sure they have covered everything, some writers like to use a checklist when they rework their drafts to improve the content, organization, and expression of ideas. If you are such a writer, the following checklist may help. The advantage of the checklist is that it helps you proceed in an orderly way, and it keeps you from overlooking some of the revision concerns. In addition, you can combine this checklist with reader response by asking a reliable reader to apply the checklist to your draft.

Content

1. Does your writing have a clear thesis, either stated or implied, that accurately presents your focus?
2. Does every point in your writing clearly relate to that thesis?
3. Are all your generalizations, including your thesis, adequately supported?
4. Are all your points well suited to your audience and purpose?
5. Have you avoided stating the obvious?
6. Does your introduction create interest in your topic?
7. Does your conclusion provide a satisfying ending?

Organization

1. Do your ideas follow logically one to the next?
2. Do your paragraphs follow logically one to the next?
3. Do the details in each paragraph relate to the topic sentence?
4. Have you used transitions to show how ideas relate to each other?
5. Have you outlined?

Expression

1. When you read your work aloud, does everything sound all right?
2. Have you avoided wordiness?
3. Have you eliminated cliches (overworked expressions)?
4. Have you used specific words?
5. Did you use a variety of sentence openers?
6. Did you use ITTS as needed?

▶ TRUST YOUR INSTINCTS

A good way to decide what needs to be changed is to read your draft over and listen to your instincts. When your instincts tell you that something is wrong, you can be reasonably sure that you have come across a problem. Even if you cannot give the problem a name, and even if you are not yet sure what change needs to be made, when you get that vague feeling that all is not well, assume that you have identified a portion of the draft that needs to be reworked. Most of the time, a writer's instincts are correct.

▶ DO NOT EDIT PREMATURELY

Sometimes writers have trouble deciding what to change because they get bogged down checking for commas, spelling, fragments, and the like. However, concerns such as these are matters of correctness, and matters of correctness are best dealt with later, during editing. During revision, you stand a better chance of recognizing what needs to be changed if you focus on content, organization, and effective expression; do not be distracted by editing concerns too early in the writing process.

▶ USE A COMPUTER

If you wrote your draft on a computer, the following tips may help you decide what changes to make.

Study a Print Copy of Your Draft   When trying to decide what changes to make in your draft, you may be better off printing out your draft and studying the print copy. Viewing the text on the screen can be less helpful because you see such small portions at a time that you may have trouble getting a good overview of your writing.

Put a Checklist in a Window   If your computer allows you to split the screen, place a revising checklist in a window to refer to as you reread your work. This way, you will be constantly reminded of what to consider while revising.

Highlight Areas with Boldface Type   If you are unsure about parts of your draft—if you don't know whether or not they should be changed—use the boldface function of your word processing program to highlight the areas in question. Then print out your draft and give it to two or more reliable readers and ask them to react to the parts in boldface type.

"My Draft Is
Too Short."

Sometimes you think you have enough ideas to get under way, so you start drafting. Later, you come to the end and place a period after your last sentence. Then you look back over your work, and you come to a disheartening recognition: Your draft is much too short, and you've already said everything you can think of. What do you do? No, you do not throw yourself in front of a high-speed train. Instead, you try one of the strategies in this chapter.

▶ UNDERLINE MAJOR POINTS

Your draft may be too short because you wrote down your major points but neglected to develop them. To determine if this is the case, go through your draft and underline every major point. Then check to see how much you have written after each underlined point. If one underlined point is immediately followed by another underlined point, you have neglected to develop an idea. Adding supporting detail after one or more of your major points can solve your length problem.

When you add detail, be careful not to state the obvious or provide unrelated information, or you will be guilty of padding—writing useless material just to bulk up the piece. Padding is a problem because it irritates readers by requiring them to read unnecessary material. Let's assume that you are writing an essay that explains how schools foster competition, rather than cooperation, in students. If you were to say that schools have students compete for grades, compete for positions on sports teams, compete for student government, compete for scholarships, and compete for cheerleading, you would be providing helpful examples that illustrate your point.

However, if you were to give a dictionary definition of *competition* as "the act of struggling to win some prize, honor, or advantage," you would be padding your essay with information your reader already knows.

▶ SHOW AFTER YOU TELL

If your draft is too short, you may be *telling* your reader things are true without *showing* that they are true. A good rule to remember is "show; don't just tell." Consider the following:

> I have always hated winter. For one thing, the cold bothers me. For another, daily living becomes too difficult.

The previous sentences are an example of telling without showing. Here is a revision with detail added to *show:*

> I have always hated winter. For one thing, the cold bothers me. Even in the house with the furnace running, I can never seem to get warm. I wear a turtleneck under a heavy wool sweater and drink one cup of hot tea after another in a futile effort to ease the chill that goes to my bones. A simple trip to the mailbox at the street leaves me chattering for an hour. My hands go numb, and my nose and ears sting from the cold. The doctor explained that I cannot tolerate the cold because I have a circulation problem which causes my capillaries to spasm, interrupting the blood flow to my extremities. I also hate winter because daily living becomes too difficult. Snow and ice are tracked into the house, necessitating frequent cleanups. Snow must be shoveled to get the car out of the driveway. Icy walks make walking treacherous, and driving to the grocery store becomes a dangerous endeavor thanks to slick, snow-covered roads.

See the difference showing—instead of just telling—can make?

▶ RETURN TO IDEA GENERATION

Your draft may be too short because you began writing before you generated enough ideas to write about. This is really not a problem; simply interrupt your drafting for a while and go back to generating ideas. If you have a favorite idea generation technique, try it now. If it lets you down, try one or more other techniques. Writers frequently step back to idea generation before going forward, so interrupting your drafting is not something you should either resist or worry about.

▶ CHECK YOUR THESIS

If you have tried the previous techniques for fleshing out your draft, and you still do not have enough material, study your thesis to see if it too severely limits the territory you can cover in your draft. If possible, broaden the thesis a bit so that you can cover more ground and thereby increase the length of your draft. Let's say, for example, that your draft has this thesis:

High school athletics teaches adolescents to be self-reliant.

If you have exhausted everything you can say about how high school athletics teaches self-reliance, if you have tried all the techniques in this chapter, and if you still only have a page and a half of material, consider expanding your thesis to allow discussion of other points:

High school athletics teaches adolescents to be self-reliant. Interestingly, however, athletics also teaches young people how to be team players.

Now the writer can expand the draft by discussing two advantages of high school athletics rather than one.

A word of caution is in order here: Do not get carried away when you expand your thesis, or you will be forced into covering too much territory. Consider how difficult it would be to provide an adequately detailed discussion of this expanded thesis:

High school athletics teaches adolescents everything they need to know to succeed as adults: how to be self-reliant, how to be a team player, how to function under pressure, how to accept criticism, and how to give 100 percent.

An essay with this thesis is destined to fail in one of two ways. Either it will be so long that the reader will feel overwhelmed, or it will provide only superficial treatment of the main points.

▶ USE A COMPUTER

Go through your draft, and before each of your main points press the insert key and then hit the space bar ten times. This should visually separate each main point and its support. Once each main point and support are separated from the rest of the essay, you can study each one individually to determine if you can add an example, a story, or some description. After adding detail to develop the main points, rejoin your sentences to form a longer draft.

"My Writing Seems Boring."

"I couldn't put it down!" "A real page-turner!" "A must read!" No, these are not the exclamations people must make about your writing, but you must hold your reader's interest or you may fail to communicate your message. If your draft seems boring, try the strategies described in this chapter.

▶ REPLACE GENERAL WORDS WITH SPECIFIC ONES

To make your writing more interesting, replace general words with more specific ones. Here are two sentences. The first has general words, which are underlined; the second has specific words, which are also underlined. Which sentence is more interesting?

> **General words:**   The car went down the street.

> **Specific words:**   The red Corvette streaked down Dover Avenue.

You probably found the second sentence more interesting because of its more specific word choice. To make your sentences more interesting, go through your draft and circle every general word. Then replace some of those words with more specific words or phrases. The following chart will give you a clearer idea of the difference between general and specific words.

General	Specific	General	Specific
car	1989 Buick	dog	mangy collie
sweater	yellow cardigan	hat	Phillies cap
shoes	Nike hightops	movie	*Field of Dreams*
feel good	feel optimistic	book	*Misery*
walk	saunter	drink	slurp
cry	sob loudly	said	snapped suddenly
house	two-story colonial	rain	pounding rain
a lot	twelve	later	in two days

▶ ADD DESCRIPTION

Description can add vitality and interest to writing, so if your draft seems boring, look for opportunities to describe something: a scene, a person's clothing, someone's facial expression, a tone of voice, the brightness of the sun, the feel of a handshake. The description need not be elaborate, nor should it distract the reader from your main point. However, carefully chosen description at appropriate points can keep your reader interested. For example, if you are telling the story of your first encounter with your advisor, some description can add liveliness:

> The door was open and I saw Dr. Harkness hunched over his desk, his nose on the paper he was studying, his eyes squinted into slits. I knocked on the door frame to get his attention, but the barely perceptible sound was too much for him. He jerked upright, startled by the intrusion. When he saw me, he brushed wisps of white hair from his eyes, smoothed his red and blue flannel shirt, and smiled sheepishly. "How can I help you, young man?" he asked, as he lifted his bulky frame from the chair.

▶ ADD SPECIFIC EXAMPLES

Examples add interest because they take the general and make it specific. So if your draft seems boring, look for opportunities to follow a general point with a specific example. In other words, don't just *say* something is true; *show* that it is true with an example. If you say that Lee is a scatterbrain, go on to show this by giving the example of the time Lee locked the keys in the car three times in one day.

▶ TELL A STORY

Another way to add vitality and interest is to tell a brief story. In addition, a story can help establish a point by serving as an example. For instance, assume you are explaining that being a student *and* a parent can get very complicated. And assume that one point you make is that sometimes the two roles conflict with each other. To establish this point, you could tell the story of the time your six-year-old woke up sick three hours before your history exam and you had to get her to the doctor, arrange for a baby sitter, and pick up a prescription—and still make it to class on time.

▶ REWRITE CLICHÉS

Clichés are tired, overworked expressions. At one time they were fresh and interesting, but because of overuse, they have become boring. A list of cliches could go on and on, but the following is a representative sampling:

cold as ice	free as a bird	sadder but wiser
high as a kite	last but not least	old as the hills
fresh as a daisy	stiff as a board	hard as nails
under the weather	bull in a china shop	raining cats and dogs
in the same boat	the last straw	smart as a whip

If your draft seems boring, reread it looking for clichés. Each time you find one, underline it. Then to add interest, replace the clichés with original phrasings. Here's an example:

Cliché: After failing algebra, Dale and I were in the same boat. We had to find a tutor—fast.

Revision: After failing algebra, Dale and I faced a similar challenge. We had to find a tutor—fast.

▶ ELIMINATE STATEMENTS OF THE OBVIOUS

When we draft, we can be so concerned with having enough material that we state obvious points. However, stating the obvious can make an otherwise strong piece of writing seem boring. Let's say that you are arguing that young people should not be permitted to watch more than an hour of television a day. A sentence like the following is likely to bore a reader because some of what it says is so obvious it does not need to be said at all.

Television, an electronic device for bringing sound and pictures into the home, can be a positive or negative influence on our children, depending on how it is used.

To make your writing more interesting, eliminate statements of the obvious:

Television can be a positive or negative influence on our children, depending on how it is used.

If your thesis takes in too much territory, you can be forced into a superficial, general discussion—and such discussions are boring. For example, consider this thesis:

> SRU is a fine university because of its quality instruction, competitive athletics, and varied campus activities.

An essay that adequately covers the university's instruction, athletics, and activities is likely to involve a superficial discussion because anything in depth will lead to a very long piece.

If your writing is boring because your discussion is too general, look at what you are trying to cover. If your thesis is ambitious, pare it down, like this:

> SRU is a fine university because of its varied campus activities.

Now you can provide a much more interesting discussion because you can give specifics and still have a piece that is a manageable length.

Use your word processing program's search-and-replace function to find general words you are in the habit of using. For example, you can ask the computer to spot where you have used these general words: *very, quite, a lot, rather, really, great, good, bad,* and *some.* Once the computer has located these words, you can decide whether to retain one or more of them or rewrite to be more specific.

"My Writing Sounds Choppy"

Read this paragraph out loud. It sounds choppy. The style seems immature. The writing does not sound like it was written by a forty-two-year-old woman with a couple of college degrees. It sounds like it was written by someone's kid brother. This is my way of showing that choppiness is bad. Is it working?

Actually, you do not always have to read your work aloud to detect choppiness. When you read silently, the words "sound" in your brain, allowing you to "hear" this problem. Once you detect choppiness, you can eliminate it with the techniques described in this chapter.

▶ USE DIFFERENT SENTENCE OPENERS

Your writing will sound choppy or singsong if too many sentences in a row all begin in the same way. For example, the first paragraph of this chapter sounds choppy because most of the sentences begin with the subject. The solution to the problem is to mix up sentence openings by trying some of the suggestions that follow.

1. **Open with a descriptive word (a modifier).**

   <u>Strangely</u>, little Billy did not enjoy his birthday.

   <u>Confused</u>, the stranger asked directions to the nearest hotel.

   <u>Melting</u>, the ice formed slushy puddles on the pavement.

2. **Open with a descriptive phrase (a modifier).**

   <u>Despite my better judgment</u>, I bought a ticket for the roller coaster ride.

   <u>Hiding in the living room</u>, twelve of us waited for the right moment to leap out and yell, "Surprise!

Pleased by her grade on the physics exam, Loretta treated herself to a special dinner.

Under the couch, the wet dog hid from her owner.

3. **Open with a subordinate clause (a dependent word group with a subject and verb).**

When Congress announced its budget reform package, members of both political parties offered their support.

If the basketball team can recruit a power forward, we will have all the ingredients for a winning season.

Before you contribute to a charity, check the identification of the person requesting the money.

4. **Open with to and the verb (an infinitive).**

To protect our resources, we must make recycling a way of life.

To convince my parents to buy me a car, I had to agree to pay the car insurance.

To gain five pounds by the start of wrestling season, Luis doubled his intake of carbohydrates.

5. **Open with the subject.**

Losses lead gains in today's stock market activity.

Lee's goal is to become the youngest manager in the company's history.

The curtains were dulled by years of accumulated dirt.

▶ VARY THE PLACEMENT OF TRANSITIONS

Transitions are words and phrases that link ideas and show how they relate to each other. One way to eliminate choppiness is to mix up your placement of transitions in your sentences.

Transition at the beginning: In addition, providing child care on campus is a good idea because more women will be able to attend classes.

Transition in the middle: Jan's opinion, on the other hand, is that child-care programs will cost the university too much money.

Transition at the end: The university's board of trustees has not made up its mind, however.

When you hear choppiness, look to see if you have two or more short sentences in a row. If so, combine at least two of those short sentences into a longer one, using one of these words:

and	nor	yet
but	for	because
or	so	

Short sentences (choppy): The house was well constructed. It was decorated badly.

Combined sentence (smoother): The house was well constructed, but it was decorated badly.

Short sentences (choppy): The fraternity and sorority both needed money. They combined their resources in a fund-raiser.

Combined sentence (smoother): The fraternity and sorority both needed money, so they combined their resources in a fund-raiser.

► FOLLOW LONG SENTENCES WITH
SHORT ONES AND SHORT SENTENCES
WITH LONG ONES

The following examples alternate long and short sentences. As you read them, notice how well they flow as a result of the variation in length.

Short followed by long: The coach jumped to his feet. Although he had been coaching football for over twenty-five years, he had never before seen such a perfectly executed play.

Long followed by short: This city needs a mayor who knows how to deal effectively with city council and how to trim waste from the municipal budget. This city needs Dale Fletcher.

► USE YOUR EAR

A good way to discover if parts of your writing are choppy is to read aloud with a pen in your hand. Where you hear that your writing is not flowing well, place a check mark. Then go back and try the techniques described in this chapter to ease the flow where you have placed the check marks.

You may find it easier to check the length of your sentences and how they open if you view them in isolation. Use the insert function of your word processing program to add six spaces before and after each sentence in your draft. With your sentences separated from each other, you can check length and openings and revise as necessary. When done, just delete the extra spaces to bring your sentences back together again.

Editing

Errors in grammar, spelling, punctuation, and capitalization present a special problem because if you make too many of these errors, your reader will become distracted and annoyed enough to lose confidence in your ability. For this reason, you have a responsibility to find and correct your mistakes. This process is editing. *For most writers, it makes sense to edit last, after all the other changes are made. This way you aren't checking something that you ultimately strike from the paper anyway.*

"I Have Trouble Finding My Mistakes."

You worked hard. You finished your piece, so off it goes to your reader. But when your reader returns your writing, you feel deflated because eagle-eye reader found lots of mistakes you never noticed. On closer look, you become frustrated because you now see the same mistakes yourself. Why does that misspelled word leap out at you now when it went unnoticed before? Why is that incorrect verb form so obvious now when it was invisible earlier?

The truth is, writers often overlook their mistakes if they do not take special pains to find them. However, the techniques in this chapter can help.

▶ EDIT LAST

The most efficient time to edit (find and correct mistakes) is near the end of your writing process, after you have made your revisions in content, organization, and wording. If you edit earlier than this, you may do extra work for nothing, such as look up the spelling of a word that you later eliminate during revision.

Also, you may have trouble finding your mistakes if you edit too soon, when your mind is really concerned with larger matters. For example, locating and eliminating sentence fragments is difficult at the same time you are concerned about supporting a point. Thus, if you have trouble finding your mistakes, be sure you save editing for last, when you can focus all your concentration on it.

▶ LEAVE YOUR WORK FOR A WHILE

By the time you are ready to look for errors, you will have spent a significant amount of time on your writing. In fact, you will be so close to it that you may not have a fresh enough perspective to notice mistakes. To compensate for this fact, you should leave your writing for a day to clear your head. When you return to your work, you should have a sharper eye for spotting mistakes.

▶ POINT TO EACH WORD AND PUNCTUATION MARK

To find your mistakes, you must go over your writing *very* slowly. If you build up even a little speed, you will probably overlook errors because you will see what you *intended* to write rather than what you actually *did* write. This is because you know so well what you want to say that you tend to see it on the page whether it is there or not. A good way to ensure that you move slowly is to point to each word and punctuation mark and study each one a second or two. Be sure that you are reading what you are pointing to; it is tempting to move your finger or pen ahead of what you are reading, which causes you to build up too much speed and miss mistakes.

▶ USE A RULER

Place a ruler under the first line of your writing and examine that line one word at a time for mistakes. Then drop the ruler down a line and examine that line for mistakes. If you move through your entire piece of writing this way, you may have better luck finding errors for two reasons. First, you are less likely to build up too much speed and miss mistakes. Second, the ruler prevents the words below the line from entering your visual field and distracting you.

▶ PREPARE A FRESH, TYPED COPY OF YOUR DRAFT

Because handwriting can be hard on the eyes, errors can be spotted more easily in typed copy. So type your draft before editing it. Also, you can be more objective about typed copy because it seems more like printed material—more like someone else's writing.

▶ LISTEN TO YOUR DRAFT

Sometimes you can hear mistakes that you overlook visually. For this reason, you should listen to your writing. Have someone read your draft to you, or read it aloud to yourself, or speak it into a tape recorder and play back the tape. If you read your draft to yourself or into a tape recorder, be sure to read *exactly* what is on the page. Remember, writers tend to read what they *meant* to say rather than what they *did* say. Also, remember that some mistakes, such as certain misspellings, cannot be heard, so listening should be combined with one or more of the visual editing strategies.

▶ LEARN YOUR PATTERN OF ERROR

We all make mistakes, but we do not all make the *same* mistakes. One person may misspell words often, another may write run-on sentences, another may have trouble choosing the correct verb, and so on. Be aware of the kinds of mistakes you make so you can make a special effort to locate those errors. In fact, edit one extra time for each of the mistakes you have a tendency to make.

Once you know the kinds of mistakes you make, you may even be able to determine under what circumstances you make those mistakes. For example, once you discover that you have trouble choosing verbs, a little study of your writing may tell you that you have this trouble whenever you begin a sentence with *there is* or *there are.* This is valuable information because it tells you to check the verbs in any sentences that begin with these words.

To tune-in to your pattern of error, keep a log of your mistakes so you can check which ones occur with the greatest frequency. If you keep a journal, you can record on a back page the kinds of mistakes you make by checking the instructor comments on your evaluated essays.

▶ USE AN EDITING CHECKLIST

One way to be sure you are editing thoroughly is to use a checklist. The one below may meet your needs. Or if you prefer, devise your own checklist of errors you are in the habit of making.

1. Have you read your work aloud to listen for problems?
2. Did you check every possible misspelling in a dictionary or with a spell checker?
3. Did you edit for run-on sentences?

4. Did you edit for sentence fragments?
5. Did you check your use of verbs?
6. Did you check your use of pronouns?
7. Did you check your use of modifiers?
8. Have you checked any punctuation you are unsure of?
9. Have you checked your use of capital letters?

▶ TRUST YOUR INSTINCTS

Maybe you have had this experience: You have a nagging feeling that something is wrong. However, you cannot give the problem a name, and you are not sure how to solve it, so you just skip over it and hope your reader does not notice. Then you submit your writing, and sure enough—your reader was troubled by the same thing you were troubled by. If you have had this experience, you learned that your instincts are reliable. When that nagging feeling tells you a problem exists, you should trust the feeling and assume that something is wrong. Because you have been using the language for many years, much of what you know has been internalized. Thus, an inner alarm may sound when you have made a mistake. Always heed that alarm, even if you are not sure what the problem is or how to solve it. Get help if necessary for diagnosing and eliminating the error.

▶ EDIT MORE THAN ONCE

Because it is so easy to overlook errors, you should edit more than once. Many writers like to edit once for anything they can find and a separate time for each of the kinds of errors they have a tendency to make.

▶ LEARN THE RULES

You cannot edit confidently if you do not know the rules. Many people think the grammar and usage rules are understood only by English teachers, but the truth is that anyone can learn them. Invest in a grammar book, and each time you make an error, study the appropriate rule so that mistake does not happen again.

▶ GET SOME HELP

Professional writers have editors who locate and correct errors that get by them, and you can get some help too. Ask someone to go over your writing to find mistakes that you overlooked. Be sure, however, that the person who helps you edit is someone who knows grammar and usage rules; otherwise, you will not get reliable information. If your school has a writing center, you may be able to stop in there for reliable editing assistance. Please keep in mind, though, that the ultimate responsibility for editing is yours. You must learn and apply the rules on your own, with only backup help from others.

► USE A COMPUTER

The techniques described below may help you edit with the aid of your computer.

Put Your Editing Checklist into a Window If your program allows you to split your screen, try placing your editing checklist into a window. Consult the checklist as you edit.

Quadruple-Space Your Text After revising, reformat your text with four spaces between each line. This way, you can edit one line at a time with less of your text entering your visual field to distract you from the words you are studying.

Edit the Screen and the Typed Copy Edit twice. The first time through, edit by studying the words on the screen, making the necessary changes as you go. Then print your text and edit a second time on the paper copy. Enter these changes into your file and print a fresh copy.

"I Used a Period and Capital Letter, so Why Isn't This a Sentence?"

From our earliest years in school, we have been taught to mark the start of a sentence with a capital letter and the end of a sentence with a period, question mark, or exclamation point. But sometimes we carry that advice too far: We take a *piece* of a sentence, add a capital, place a period, and call what we get a whole sentence. However, a piece of a sentence (even with a capital letter and period added) is still just a *piece*—it is not a whole sentence. Instead, it is a sentence *fragment*. Here is an example of a sentence followed by a fragment:

Sentence followed by fragment:	Dale has many admirable traits. Such as loyalty, creativity, and integrity.
Explanation	Despite the period and capital, *such as loyalty, creativity, and integrity* is only a piece of a sentence and does not have sentence status.
Fragment eliminated:	Dale has many admirable traits, such as loyalty, creativity, and integrity.
Explanation:	The fragment is eliminated by joining it to the sentence.

If you have trouble editing for sentence fragments, the tips in the rest of this chapter should help you.

▶ ISOLATE EVERYTHING YOU ARE CALLING A SENTENCE

Start at the beginning of your draft and place one finger of your left hand under the capital letter. Then place a finger of your right hand under the

46

period, question mark, or exclamation point. Now read the word group between your fingers out loud. Does it sound as if something is missing? If not, you probably have a legitimate sentence. If so, then you probably have a sentence fragment.

Move through your entire draft this way, isolating word groups with your fingers and reading out loud. Each time you hear a fragment, stop and make the necessary correction. This procedure is time-consuming, but the payoff is worth the investment of time.

▶ READ YOUR DRAFT BACKWARD

A good way to find fragments is to read your draft backward. Simply begin by reading the last sentence; pause for a moment to hear if something is missing, and then read the next-to-the-last sentence, again pausing to listen for something missing. Proceed this way until you have worked back to the first sentence. Each time you hear that something is missing, stop and correct the fragment you have found.

▶ CHECK -ING AND -ED VERB FORMS

Sometimes sentence fragments result when *-ing* or *-ed* verb forms stand by themselves. Here are two examples with the *-ing* and *-ed* verb forms underlined.

Fragment: The kitten stretching after her nap.

Fragment: The child frustrated by the complicated toy.

To correct fragments that result when -ing or -ed verbs stand alone, pick an appropriate verb from this list and add it to the -ing or -ed form:

is	was	have	had
are	were	has	

Fragment: The kitten stretching after her nap.

Sentence: The kitten was stretching after her nap.

Sentence: The kitten is stretching after her nap.

Fragment: The child frustrated by the complicated toy.

Sentence: The child is frustrated by the complicated toy.

Sentence: The child was frustrated by the complicated toy.

To find fragments that result when -ing or -ed verbs stand alone, go through your draft checking each -ing and -ed verb form. Read the sentence with the form and ask if a verb from the above list is necessary for a sense of completeness.

▶ CHECK FOR FRAGMENT WARNING WORDS

The following words often begin sentence fragments:

after	because	such as
although	especially	when
as	even though	whenever
as if	for example	unless
as long as	if	until
as soon as	in order to	while
as though	since	
before	so that	

To find fragments in your writing, read aloud every word group that begins with one of the above words or phrases and listen carefully to hear if something is missing. Do not assume that anything beginning with one of these fragment warning words is automatically a sentence fragment because sentences, too, can begin with these words and phrases. To be sure, read aloud to hear if something is missing.

Sentence: While Dale cleaned the house, Lee cooked dinner. (When you read these words out loud, there is no sense that something is missing.)

Fragment: While Dale cleaned the house. (When you read these words out loud, you can hear that something is missing.)

▶ WATCH OUT FOR WHO, WHOM, WHOSE, WHICH, AND WHERE

If you begin a word group with *who, whom, whose, which,* or *where* without asking a question, you have most likely written a sentence fragment.

Sentence: Who lives next door?

Fragment: Who lives next door.

Sentence: Whose advice have I valued over the years?

Fragment: Whose advice I have valued over the years.

To find fragments, look at any word group that begins with *who, whom, whose, which,* or *where* and be sure that word group is asking a question. If it is not, join the word group to the sentence before it, as illustrated here:

Sentence and fragment:	Lee is a good friend. <u>Whose advice I have valued over the years.</u>
Sentence:	Lee is a good friend, whose advice I have valued over the years.

► ELIMINATE THE FRAGMENTS

The techniques just described will help you locate sentence fragments; the two techniques that follow will help you eliminate fragments once you find them. Keep in mind, however, that each technique will not work for every fragment, so if one correction method does not work, try the other.

Join the Fragment to a Sentence before or after It

Sentence and fragment:	The cruise ship moved slowly into the harbor. <u>While the passengers waved from the upper deck.</u>
Fragment joined to sentence:	The cruise ship moved slowly into the harbor, while the passengers waved from the upper deck.
Fragment and sentence:	<u>While trying on the cashmere sweater.</u> Molly snagged the sleeve with her class ring.
Fragment joined to sentence:	While trying on the cashmere sweater, Molly snagged the sleeve with her class ring.

Add the Missing Word or Words

A fragment that results when a word or words are left out (usually the subject or part of the verb) can be eliminated with the addition of the missing word or words.

Sentence and fragment:	The auto mechanic assured us the repairs would be minor. <u>Then proceeded to list a dozen things wrong with the car.</u>
Fragment eliminated with addition of the subject *he*:	The auto mechanic assured us the repairs would be minor. Then he proceeded to list a dozen things wrong with the car.
Fragment:	The unhappy toddler pouting in the corner.
Fragment eliminated with the addition of part of the verb (*was*):	The unhappy toddler was pouting in the corner.

Sentence and fragment:	I would like to go to the county fair. <u>But not without you</u>.
Fragment eliminated with addition of subject and verb:	I would like to go to the county fair. But I do not want to go without you.

▶ USE A COMPUTER

The key to finding fragments in your writing is to isolate every word group you are calling a sentence; then check to be sure each of them *really is* a sentence. The computer can help you isolate. Simply insert eight spaces before each capital letter that marks the start of a sentence. Then read each word group separately to hear if something is missing. Because each word group is now physically separated, finding fragments can be easier. When you are done with this aspect of editing, reformat your text to draw everything back together.

"How Can This Be a Run-On? It's Not Even Long."

One of the most frequently occurring editing errors is the run-on sentence (sometimes called the "comma splice" or "fused sentence"). So if you have been told that you write run-ons, know that you have plenty of company.

A *run-on sentence* occurs when two word groups that can be sentences (independent clauses) stand without the proper separation. Here are two word groups that can be sentences (independent clauses):

1. every night the team studied together for two hours
2. by the end of the semester, everyone's grades improved

A run-on is created when these independent clauses are not properly separated:

Run-on: Every night the team studied together for two hours by the end of the semester, everyone's grades improved.

To eliminate the run-on, the independent clauses can be separated three ways:

1. With a comma and coordinate conjunction (<u>and, but, or, nor, for, so, yet</u>)

Every night the team studied together for two hours<u>, and</u> by the end of the semester, everyone's grades improved.

2. With a semicolon (;)

Every night the team studied together for two hours<u>;</u> by the end of the semester, everyone's grades improved.

3. With a period and capital letter

Every night the team studied together for two hours. By the end of the semester everyone's grades improved.

A run-on sentence occurs when you do not separate independent clauses in one of the above three ways.

Run-on: Every night the team studied together for two hours by the end of the semester everyone's grades improved. (There is no separation between the independent clauses.)

Run-on: Every night the team studied together for two hours, by the end of the semester, everyone's grades improved. (Only a comma separates the independent clauses; no coordinate conjunction appears.)

Run-on: Every night the team studied together for two hours, thus by the end of the semester everyone's grades improved. (*Thus* is not a coordinate conjunction.)

The rest of this chapter describes ways to find run-on sentences in your writing.

▶ STUDY SENTENCES INDIVIDUALLY

One way to find run-ons is to study each of your sentences separately. Place one finger of your left hand under the capital letter and one finger of your right hand under the period, question mark, or exclamation point. Then identify the number of independent clauses (word groups that can stand as sentences) between your fingers. If you have one, the sentence is fine. If you have two or more, look to see what is separating the clauses. If a semicolon separates the independent clauses, the sentence is fine; if a comma and coordinate conjunction (*and, but, or, nor, for, so, yet*) separates the independent clauses, the sentence is fine. However, if nothing separates the independent clauses, or if only a comma separates the independent clauses, then you have a run-on.

When you identify a run-on, you can eliminate it by separating the independent clauses in one of three ways:

1. With a comma and coordinate conjunction
2. With a semicolon
3. With a period and capital letter

Move through your whole draft this way checking for and eliminating run-ons. Although time-consuming, this procedure is very effective.

► CIRCLE COMMAS

To find the special kind of run-on called the *comma splice,* go through your draft and circle every comma. Then go back to your first comma and identify what you have before it and what you have after it. If you have an independent clause (a word group that can be a sentence) on *both* sides, make sure you have a coordinate conjunction *(and, but, or, nor, for, so, yet)* after the comma. If your independent clauses are not separated by one of these words (or the word *because*), then add one of them.

► UNDERLINE RUN-ON WARNING WORDS

When you edit for run-ons, pay special attention to these words:

he	however	then	moreover	nevertheless
she	therefore	thus	furthermore	similarly
it	hence	finally	consequently	next
they	as a result	in addition	on the contrary	for example

Read over your draft and underline any of these warning words that appear. Then check to see what is on *both* sides of each underlined word. If an independent clause (a word group that can be a sentence) is on *both* sides, place a semicolon (not a comma) before the warning word.

► FORGET ABOUT LONG AND SHORT

Many people think that a long sentence is sure to be a run-on. Similarly, they think that a short sentence cannot possibly be one. This thinking is mistaken, for length is not a factor. The only factor is how independent clauses are separated, so when you edit for run-ons, forget about how long or short your sentences are.

► USE A COMPUTER

The strategies that follow will help you locate run-on sentences using computer technology.

Search for Warning Words One way to edit for run-ons with a computer is to use the search function to find all the run-on warning words (*however, therefore, thus,* etc.). Once these words are identified in your text, check for independent clauses on both sides of these words. Wherever you find independent clauses on *both sides* of a warning word, be sure you have a semicolon before the word.

Isolate Sentences Insert eight spaces before every capital letter marking the beginning of a sentence. This will visually separate your sentences from each other, making it easier to study sentences individually. After finding and eliminating run-ons, reformat your text to bring everything back together.

"I/Me, She/Her, He/Him, They/Them, We/Us— What's the Difference?"

There you are writing along merrily, and then it happens—you have to use a pronoun and you're not sure which one is correct: Did the police officer issue the warning to Lee and me or to Lee and I? "Lee and me; no, it's Lee and I; no, wait, Lee and me." Ah, what the heck—you pick one and hope for the best.

Writers often stumble over pronouns, but the next time you are unsure, try the procedures in this chapter.

► CROSS OUT EVERYTHING IN THE PHRASE
  BUT THE PRONOUN

When a pronoun is linked with a noun, you may not be sure which pronoun to use. Is it "Sally and I" or "Sally and me"? Is it "the boys and us" or "the boys and we"? When in doubt, cross out everything in the phrase but the pronoun and read what is left:

~~My brothers and~~ I saw *Batman* six times.

~~My brothers and~~ me saw *Batman* six times.

With everything but the pronoun crossed out, you can tell that the correct choice is *I:*

My brothers and I saw *Batman* six times.

Here is another example:

Dr. Cohen lent ~~Maria and~~ I a copy of the book.

Dr. Cohen lent ~~Maria and~~ me a copy of the book.

With everything but the pronoun crossed out, you can tell that the correct choice is *me:*

> Dr. Cohen lent Maria and me a copy of the book.

▶ CROSS OUT WORDS THAT RENAME

Sometimes words follow a pronoun and rename it. These words that rename are called *appositives.*

We baseball players:	*Baseball players* follows the pronoun and renames it.
Us sophomores:	*Sophomores* follows the pronoun and renames it.
You sports fans:	*Sports fans* follows the pronoun and renames it.

To make pronoun choice easier, cross out the words that rename (the appositives):

> We ~~spectators~~ jumped to our feet and cheered when the band took the field.
>
> Us ~~spectators~~ jumped to our feet and cheered when the band took the field.

With the appositive crossed out, the correct choice is clear:

> We spectators jumped to our feet and cheered when the band took the field.

Here is another example:

> Loud rock music can be irritating to we ~~older folks~~.
>
> Loud rock music can be irritating to us ~~older folks~~.

With the appositive crossed out, the correct choice is clear:

> Loud rock music can be irritating to us older folks.

▶ ADD THE MISSING WORDS IN
  COMPARISONS

Which is it: "Bev is a better foul shooter than I" or "Bev is a better foul shooter than me"? To find out, add the unstated comparison word:

> Bev is a better foul shooter than I am.
>
> Bev is a better foul shooter than me am.

With the missing word added, you can tell that the correct pronoun is *I:*

> Bev is a better foul shooter than I.

Here is another example:

> John Jakes's new novel interested Miguel as much as I.

John Jakes's new novel interested Miguel as much as me.

To decide on the correct pronoun, add the missing words:

John Jakes's new novel interested Miguel as much as it interested me.

John Jakes's new novel interested Miguel as much as it interested I.

With the missing comparison words added, you can tell that the correct pronoun is *me.*

► CIRCLE <u>THEY</u>, <u>THEIR</u>, AND <u>THEM</u>, AND DRAW AN ARROW TO THE NOUNS THEY REFER TO

They, their, and *them* refer to plural nouns:

All students should bring (their) notebooks to the next class; if (they) forget (them) class participation will prove difficult.

A problem occurs when *they, their,* or *them* is used to refer to a singular noun:

A person who cares about the environment will recycle.
(They) will also avoid using styrofoam and plastic.

In the previous sentence the plural *they* refers to the singular *person.* This creates a problem called *lack of agreement.* To eliminate this problem, make the pronoun and noun agree in one of these two ways:

Singular noun and pronoun: A person who cares about the environment will recycle. (He or she) will also avoid using Styrofoam and plastic.

Plural noun and pronoun: People who care about the environment will recycle. (They) will also avoid using Styrofoam and plastic.

One way to ensure agreement is to circle *they, their,* and *them* and then draw arrows to the nouns referred to. Be sure each of these pronouns refers to a plural noun. If it does not, make the noun plural or change the pronoun to a singular form.

► PAY SPECIAL ATTENTION TO <u>EVERYBODY</u>, <u>EVERYONE</u>, <u>EVERYTHING</u>, <u>SOMEBODY</u>, <u>SOMEONE</u>, <u>SOMETHING</u>, <u>ANYBODY</u>, <u>ANYONE</u>, AND <u>ANYTHING</u>

In formal usage, these nine words (called *indefinite pronouns*) are singular (*-body, -one,* and *-thing* at the end can help you remember this). Thus, pronouns that refer to these words should also be singular if you are writing for an audience that expects formal usage. Here are some examples:

> Everybody should remember *his or her* admission forms when reporting to orientation.

> Someone left *his or her* coat in the auditorium.

> Anybody who wants to bring *his or her* family may do so.

> Be sure to put everything in *its* place.

When you edit, look for these nine words. If you find one, look to see if a pronoun refers to it. If so, be sure that the pronoun is singular. Do not rely on the sound of the sentence because the plural pronoun may sound fine since it is often used in informal spoken English.

▶ CIRCLE <u>YOU</u>

The pronoun *you* addresses the reader; if it is used to refer to someone other than the reader, the result is a problem called *person shift*. To avoid this problem, circle *you* when it appears in your draft, and then draw an arrow to the word it refers to. If this word names someone other than the reader, replace *you* with the correct pronoun. Here is an example:

> Distance runners must train religiously. (You) cannot compete successfully if (you) run only on weekends.

Now here is the corrected version:

> Distance runners must train religiously. (They) cannot compete successfully if (they) run only on weekends.

▶ UNDERLINE <u>IT</u> AND <u>THEY</u> TO AVOID
UNSTATED REFERENCE

Underline *it* and *they* and then check to be sure you have supplied a noun for these words to refer to. Otherwise, you will have a problem called *unstated reference*.

Unstated reference: Charlie is a very curious child. Because of <u>it</u>, he asks questions all the time.

Explanation: <u>It</u> cannot refer to *curious* because *curious* is a modifier, not a noun. The reference is meant to be *curiosity*, but that word is not stated.

Correction: Charlie is a very curious child. Because of his curiosity, he asks questions all the time.

Unstated reference:	When I went to the unemployment office, <u>they</u> told me that some construction jobs were available.
Explanation:	There is no stated noun for <u>they</u> to refer to.
Correction:	When I went to the unemployment office, the employment counselor told me that some construction jobs were available.

▶ WATCH OUT FOR UNCLEAR REFERENCE

When a pronoun can refer to more than one noun and the reader cannot tell what the writer means, the problem is *unclear reference.*

Unclear reference:	Dad was in the garage with Brian when he heard the telephone ring.
Explanation:	Because of unclear reference, the reader can't tell whether Dad or Brian heard the phone.
Correction:	Dad was in the garage with Brian when Brian heard the telephone ring.

▶ USE A COMPUTER

The search function of your word processing program can help you check your use of some pronouns. First, use the search function to locate these pronouns in your draft: *they, their, them.* Then check to be sure that you have plural nouns for these words to refer to. Also, check to be sure *they* has a stated noun to refer to.

Next, use the search function to locate every use of *everyone, everybody, everything, someone, somebody, something, anyone, anybody,* and *anything.* Check to see if a pronoun refers to each of these words. If so, use the singular form for formal usage.

Finally, use your search function to locate every use of *you.* Then see if you need to change this pronoun because it is not really referring to the reader.

"I'm Not Sure Which Verb to Use."

A student once joked that she knows why verbs are called "action words"—because they so *actively* cause her trouble. Choosing the right verb *can* be tricky at times, but most of the problems arise in just a few special instances. Strategies for dealing with these instances are discussed in this section.

▶ CROSS OUT PHRASES BEFORE THE VERB

A phrase before the verb can trick you into choosing the wrong verb form. Consider this sentence:

The stack of books (*is* or *are?*) about to fall.

Is it *The stack is* or *The books are?* To decide, cross out the phrase *of books* to get:

The stack ~~of books~~ is about to fall.

Phrases before the verb often begin with one of these words (called *prepositions*):

about	before	in	through
above	between	into	to
across	by	like	toward
after	during	of	under
among	for	on	up
at	from	over	with

When in doubt about the correct verb form, cross out phrases beginning with one of these words. Here are some examples:

The container of old dishes (*is* or *are*?) on the landing.

The container ~~of old dishes~~ (*is* or *are*?) on the landing.

The container of old dishes is on the landing.

The herd of steers (*graze* or *grazes*?) contentedly.

The herd ~~of steers~~ (*graze* or *grazes*?) contentedly.

The herd of steers grazes contentedly.

The characteristics of the German shepherd (*make* or *makes*?) him a suitable show dog.

The characteristics ~~of the German shepherd~~ (*make* or *makes*?) him a suitable show dog.

The characteristics of the German shepherd make him a suitable show dog.

▶ REWRITE QUESTIONS

Choosing the correct verb form can be tricky in sentences that ask questions because the verb comes before the subject. Verb choice becomes much easier, however, if you rewrite the sentence so it is no longer a question. Here's an example:

Sentence with question: (*Have* or *has*?) the students finished taking exams?

Sentence rewritten: The students *have* finished taking exams.

Sentence with question and correct verb: Have the students finished taking exams?

▶ REWRITE SENTENCES BEGINNING WITH <u>HERE</u> AND <u>THERE</u>

When a sentence begins with *here* or *there,* the verb comes before the subject, which can make choosing the correct verb a little tricky. To be sure you have the correct verb, rewrite the sentence putting the subject before the verb. The correct choice should be easier that way.

Sentence with *here*: Here (*is* or *are*?) the important papers you asked for.

Sentence rewritten: The important papers you asked for are here.

Sentence with *here* and correct verb: Here are the important papers you asked for.

Sentence with _there_:	There (_was_ or _were_?) an excellent dance band playing at the wedding reception.
Sentence rewritten:	An excellent dance band was playing at the wedding reception.
Sentence with _there_ and correct verb:	There was an excellent dance band playing at the wedding reception.

▶ CIRCLE EACH, EITHER, NEITHER, ONE, NONE, ANYONE, ANYBODY, ANYTHING, EVERYONE, EVERYBODY, EVERYTHING, SOMEONE, SOMEBODY, AND SOMETHING

These words are _indefinite pronouns,_ and in formal usage they take singular verbs—even though the sense of the sentence suggests that a plural verb is logical. To check for the correct verb when you have used one of these words as the subject of a sentence, circle the word and draw an arrow to the verb. Then check that verb to be sure it is singular.

Each of the students wants (not _want_) to have the test on Friday so the weekend is more relaxing.

One of the complaints voiced at the city council meeting was (not _were_) that police response time is too slow.

Either of these literature courses fulfills (not _fulfill_) your humanities requirement.

Neither of these paintings suits (not _suit_) my taste.

None of Lee's excuses is (not _are_) believable.

Do not rely on the sound of the sentence with these words because the plural verb may sound just fine, and the singular verb may sound a little off. This is because the plural verb is often used in informal speech and writing. Nonetheless, use the singular verb for strict grammatical correctness in formal usage.

▶ LISTEN TO YOUR VERB TENSES

Tense means time. Many verbs change their form to show different tenses (times):

Present tense (time):	Today I _walk_ two miles for exercise.
Past tense (time):	Yesterday I _walked_ two miles for exercise.
Future tense (time):	Tomorrow I _will walk_ two miles for exercise.

Sometimes a change in verb tense is necessary to show a change in time, but sometimes writers change tense inappropriately and create a problem called *tense shift*.

Appropriate change in tense from past to future: When I *asked* Paul to lend me his car, he *said*, "Of course, I *will lend* it to you."

Problem tense shift from present to past: After I *finish* my homework, I *watched* a movie.

If you have a tendency to write inappropriate tense shifts, read your draft out loud and listen to your verb tenses. You are likely to hear problem shifts if you are careful to read exactly what is on the page.

"I Have Trouble with the Forms of Modifiers."

A *modifier* is a word or phrase that describes another word. For example, consider this sentence:

Terry speaks so slowly that no one takes the time to listen.

Because *slowly* describes *speaks, slowly* is a modifier. Modifiers take different forms in different grammatical settings, and if those forms give you some trouble, the suggestions in this chapter can help.

▶ DRAW AN ARROW FROM THE MODIFIER
TO THE WORD DESCRIBED

Which sentence is correct?

The party ended so *quickly* that no one had a chance to eat.

The party ended so *quick* that no one had a chance to eat.

If you are unsure, you may have trouble knowing when to use adjectives and when to use adverbs. An *adjective* describes a noun or pronoun, and an *adverb* describes a verb or other modifier. Frequently, the adverb form ends in *-ly* and the adjective form does not.

Adjectives	Adverbs
brief	briefly
swift	swiftly
loud	loudly
clear	clearly

If you are unsure which form to use, draw an arrow from the modifier to the word it describes. If the arrow is drawn to a noun or pronoun, then use the adjective form. If the arrow is drawn to a verb or modifier, then use the adverb form. Here are some examples.

Is it *quick* or *quickly* in this sentence?

Diane mowed the lawn (*quick* or *quickly*?) so she could leave with her friends.

To decide, draw an arrow from the modifier to the word described. If the word described is a noun or a pronoun, use the adjective; if it is a verb or another modifier, use the adverb (which often ends in *-ly*).

Diane mowed the lawn (*quick* or *quickly*?) so she could leave with her friends.

Now you can tell that *quickly* is called for because a verb is described:

Diane mowed the lawn quickly so she could leave with her friends.

Here are some more examples:

David was (*absolute* or *absolutely*?) sure of the answer.

David was absolutely sure of the answer. (A modifier is described, so the adverb is used.)

Chris was (*happy* or *happily*?) that the midterm examination was postponed for two days.

Chris was happy that the midterm examination was postponed for two days. (A noun is described, so the adjective is used.)

▶ REMEMBER THAT <u>GOOD</u> IS AN ADJECTIVE AND <u>WELL</u> IS AN ADVERB—WITH ONE CAUTION AND ONE EXCEPTION

1. *Good* is an adjective; it describes nouns and pronouns:
The good news is that I got the job.
2. *Well* is an adverb; it describes verbs and modifiers:
After ten years of lessons, Maxine plays the piano well.

Note: Now here's the caution:

After verbs like *taste, seem, appear,* and *look,* use *good* because the noun or pronoun before the verb is being described.

The meat tastes good, even though it is overcooked.

Claudia's appearance looks good, although she just had surgery.

The restaurant seems good, so let's eat here.

Note: Now here's the exception:

Well is used as an adjective to mean "in good health."

> After six brownies and a bottle of soda, the child did not feel well.

▶ EACH TIME YOU USE <u>MORE</u> OR <u>MOST</u>,
CHECK TO BE SURE YOU HAVE NOT USED
AN <u>-ER</u> OR <u>-EST</u> FORM

Yes: I like tacos *better* than nachos.

No: I like tacos *more better* than nachos.

Yes: Mike and Janet are *happiest* at the beach.

No: Mike and Janet are *most happiest* at the beach.

Yes: You must be *more careful,* or you will be hurt.

No: You must be *more carefuler,* or you will be hurt.

Yes: This is the *quietest* spot I know.

No: This is the *most quietest* spot I know.

▶ CHECK EVERY SENTENCE THAT OPENS
WITH AN <u>-ING</u> OR <u>-ED</u> VERB FORM

An *-ing* or *-ed* verb form can be used as an adjective:

> Whistling, Carolyn strolled through the park.

Whistling is a verb form that is used as an adjective to describe *Carolyn.*

> Carved out of marble, the statue costs thousands of dollars.

Carved is a verb form used as an adjective to describe *statue.*

When an *-ing* or *-ed* form opens a sentence, it should be followed by the word that the form describes. Otherwise the result will be a *dangling modifier.* Dangling modifiers can create some pretty silly sentences:

Dangling modifier: While making the coffee, the toast burned. (This sentence says that the toast made the coffee.)

Correction: While making the coffee, I burned the toast. (The opening *-ing* verb form is followed by a word it can sensibly describe.)

Dangling modifier: Exhausted from work, a nap was needed. (This sentence says that the nap was exhausted.)

Correction: Exhausted from work, Lucy needed a nap. (The *-ed* verb form is followed by a word it can logically describe.)

If you are in the habit of writing dangling modifiers, check every opening

-*ing* and *-ed* verb form and be sure it is closely followed by a word it can sensibly describe.

If a modifier is too far from the word it describes, the result is known as a *misplaced modifier*. A misplaced modifier can create a silly sentence:

Misplaced modifier: Lee bought a bicycle from a neighbor with a flat tire. (The sentence says that the neighbor had a flat tire.)

Correction: Lee bought a bicycle with a flat tire from a neighbor. (The modifier has been moved closer to the word it describes.)

"I Can't Spell."

There's good news and bad news. First the bad news: Misspelled words are a real problem because they lead the reader to think you are not very capable. Now the good news: Lots of very capable people do not spell well, but they have learned ways to solve their spelling problem. You, too, can eliminate misspellings if you use the techniques in this chapter.

▶ WHEN IN DOUBT, CHECK IT OUT

When it comes to using a dictionary, we all tend to be lazy. Nonetheless, the only surefire way to check a spelling is to look up the word. If you have even the slightest suspicion that a word is misspelled, check the dictionary. Remember, it does not matter how many words you misspell, as long as you correct the misspellings before your writing reaches your reader.

▶ BUY TWO DICTIONARIES

To make looking words up as convenient as possible, invest in two dictionaries. Buy one hardback collegiate dictionary to keep on your writing desk and one fat paperback to carry with you. You are more likely to look up a word if you have a dictionary at hand and do not have to get up and walk somewhere to check a spelling.

▶ USE A SPELLING DICTIONARY

Spelling dictionaries, available in most drugstores and bookstores, reference frequently misspelled words. Because they provide spellings without definitions, these volumes are thin—a fact which makes them particularly convenient to carry around. If you must look up words often, a spelling dictionary may prove less cumbersome than a standard dictionary.

▶ USE A POCKET SPELL CHECKER

Pocket spell checkers are electronic gadgets about the size of some calculators. These items can be expensive, but if you are more inclined to check spellings with an electronic gizmo than with a dictionary, they are worth every penny.

▶ LEARN CORRECT PRONUNCIATIONS

Sometimes people misspell because they pronounce a word incorrectly. For example, *February* may be misspelled if it is pronounced "Feb·u·ary"; *preventive* may be misspelled if it is pronounced "pre·ven·ta·tive." Learning to pronounce words correctly is the first step in spelling them correctly.

▶ BREAK A WORD INTO PARTS

When a word is composed of identifiable parts, spell the word out part by part. Words like the following may be more manageable when spelled out part by part:

under·stand·able	with·hold	arm·chair
room·mate	kinder·garten	dis·ease
comfort·able	lone·liness	over·coat

▶ BREAK A WORD INTO SYLLABLES

Some words are more easily spelled if you go syllable by syllable. Words of three or more syllables are often better handled this way.

or·gan·i·za·tion	cit·i·zen	mon·u·men·tal
Jan·u·ar·y	invi·ta·tion	ho·s·pi·tal
in·di·vis·i·ble	con·ver·sa·tion	pro·ba·bly

▶ LOOK FOR PREFIXES

When a prefix (word beginning) is added to a word, the spelling of the base word will probably not change.

mis·take	dis·satisfaction	mis·spell
un·nerve	un·necessary	pre·pare
mis·inform	inter·related	pre·record

▶ USE MEMORY TRICKS

Think of tricks to help you spell words you have trouble with. For example, the word *instrument* contains *strum*, and you strum a guitar, which is an instrument. Actors in a *tragedy* often *rage* at each other.

Memory tricks can be particularly helpful for pairs of words that are often mistaken for each other. You may find some of the following tricks to your liking, and you may want to make up tricks for other pairs of words that you confuse.

1. advice/advise

    a. Advice means a suggestion.

      Joel's advice proved sound.

    b. Advise means to give advice.

      Katherine is the best person to advise you.

Memory trick: A person with a vice needs advice.

2. affect/effect

    a. Affect means to influence.

      The drought will affect the economy for years to come.

    b. Effect means result.

      The effects of the drought are devastating.

Memory trick: The first syllable of effect rhymes with the first syllable of result.

3. all ready/already

    a. All ready means "all set."

      By three o'clock, the family was all ready to leave for Virginia Beach.

    b. Already means "by this time."

      We are already an hour behind schedule, and we haven't begun the trip yet.

Memory trick: All ready and all set are two words.

4. among/between

   a. Among is used for more than two.

   Divide the candy among the four children.

   b. Between is used for two.

   The difference between the ages of Phil and Harry is not important.

Memory trick: Can you fit anything between the two e's in the last syllable of between?

5. beside/besides

   a. Beside means "alongside of."

   I parked the Winnebago beside the Corvette.

   b. Besides means "in addition to."

   Besides calculus, Joyce is taking solid geometry.

Memory trick: The final s in besides is "in addition to" the first s.

6. fewer/less

   a. Fewer is for things that can be counted.

   Fewer students enrolled for spring semester than for fall semester.

   b. Less is used for things that cannot be counted.

   People who exercise regularly experience less stress than those who do not.

Memory trick: Think of countless. Less is used for things that cannot be counted.

7. passed/past

   a. Past refers to previous time. It also means "by."

   I have learned from past experience not to trust Jerry. When I drove past the house, no one was home.

   b. Passed means "went by" or "handed."

   The train passed at 60 miles per hour. Louise passed a note to Katie, but the teacher saw her and became angry.

Memory trick: Remember the p and t in past and previous time.

8. then/than

   a. Then refers to a certain time.

   The trumpets blared; then the cymbals crashed.

b. <u>Than</u> is used to compare.

I like small classes better <u>than</u> large lectures.

Memory trick: Think of the <u>e</u> in <u>then</u> and <u>time</u>; think of the <u>a</u> in <u>than</u> and <u>compare</u>.

▶ UNDERLINE WORDS TO CHECK LATER

Often as we write a word while drafting or revising, we have a sense that it is spelled wrong. Yet, looking the word up at that point is undesirable because it interrupts our drafting or revising momentum. But later we forget to look up the word or no longer realize it is misspelled, and so it remains incorrect. To solve this problem, underline every word that seems misspelled as you write it. Then you have a visual reminder to look up the word later, when it is more convenient.

▶ KEEP A SPELLING LIST

People who are serious about improving their spelling often look up the words they misspell and add the words, correctly spelled, to a list for study. Each day, they study the list and memorize another word or two in an effort to increase the number of words they know how to spell.

▶ USE A COMPUTER

Many word processing programs come with spell checkers. If yours does not, or if you desire a more powerful spell checker, you can purchase one as an add-on program.

Spell checkers test every word you've written against the words in the dictionary in the computer's memory. If a word is not recognized, the spell checker will offer alternative spellings. If the spell checker comes across a typing error, it may be baffled if nothing in its memory comes close to the spelling. In this case, it will not know what to suggest as a correct spelling. Also, homophones (soundalikes) are untouched by spell checkers, so the confusion of something like *there, their, they're* will not be resolved. However, despite these limitations, spell checkers can be helpful to people with chronic spelling problems.

23

"What Do I Do If I Want to Quote Somebody?"

From time to time, you will want to reproduce the words someone has spoken or written: Those words may advance a story; they may add vividness; they may lend insight into character; or they may provide support for an idea. No matter what motivates you to do so, when you quote someone, you are obligated to get it right. That means you must reproduce the words *exactly* as they were spoken or written, and it means you must follow the relevant punctuation and capitalization rules—the ones given in this chapter.

Punctuate and Capitalize According to Where in the Sentence the Quotation Occurs

If your quotation comes *after* the statement of who spoke, model this form:

Eli reminded us, "Put out the campfire before retiring."

If your quotation comes *before* the statement of who spoke, model this form:

"Put out the campfire before retiring," Eli reminded us.

Determine Whether the Quotation or the Entire Sentence Asks a Question

When the quotation asks a question, model one of these forms:

The reporter asked Senator McEwin, "Did you vote for the trade bill?"

"Did you vote for the trade bill?" the reporter asked Senator McEwin.

When the entire sentence asks a question, model this form:

Did the newspaper really say, "The president of the school board plans to resign"? (The question mark appears outside the quotation mark.)

Reproduce a Person's Thoughts as a Quotation

A person's thoughts are treated like spoken words, especially when a story is being told. Here is an example:

Julia thought, "It's time I made a change in my life."

Be Sure You Really Have Exact Words

Before using quotation marks, be sure you are reproducing someone's exact words.

Use quotation marks (exact words):	The police officer said, "Move your car."
Do not use quotation marks (not exact words):	The police officer said that you should move your car.

24

"I Have Trouble with Apostrophes."

Apostrophes have two main functions: They are used in contractions to take the place of missing letters, and they signal possession. Some people think apostrophes have a third function: to drive them crazy. Apostrophes *can* be pesky, so if you are unsure how to use them, try the techniques presented in this chapter.

Identify the Missing Letter(s) in a Contraction

A *contraction* is formed by taking two words, dropping one or more letters, and joining the two words into one. In contractions, discover which letter or letters are missing, and place the apostrophe at the site of the missing letter(s). For example, the contraction form of *did not* is *didn't.* Because the *o* is left out of *not,* the apostrophe is placed between the *n* and the *t.* Here are some more examples:

have + not = haven't (apostrophe at site of missing *o*)

we + will = we'll (apostrophe at site of missing *wi*)

it + is = it's (apostrophe at site of missing *i*)

✔ *NOTE: The contraction form of will not is the unusual won't.*

USE *IT'S* ONLY WHEN YOU CAN SUBSTITUTE *IT IS* OR *IT HAS*

1. ***It's* is the contraction form of *it is* or *it has*.**

    <u>It's</u> time for a change of leadership in this state.
    (<u>It is</u> time for a change of leadership in this state.)

    <u>It's</u> been 10 years since I smoked a cigarette.
    (<u>It has</u> been 10 years since I smoked a cigarette.)

2. ***Its* is a possessive form; it shows ownership and cannot be substituted for *it is* or *it has*.**

    Yes: The river overflowed <u>its</u> banks. (*Its* shows ownership.)

    No: <u>Its</u> too late to turn back now.

    Yes: <u>It's</u> too late to turn back now. (*It's* here means *it is*.)

AVOID CONTRACTIONS

No law says that you must use contractions. If you are unsure where to place the apostrophe, use the two-word form instead of the contraction.

FOR POSSESSIVE FORMS, ASK TWO QUESTIONS

Apostrophes are used with nouns to show possession. To determine how to use the apostrophe, ask, "Does the noun end in *s?*"

1. **If the noun *does not* end in *s*, add an apostrophe and an *s*, like this:**

    President + 's = President's

    The President's Council on Aging reports an increase in homelessness among the elderly.

    children + 's = children's

    Children's toys cost more money than they are worth.

2. **If the noun ends in *s*, ask, "Is the noun singular or plural?"**

    a.   If the noun is singular, add an apostrophe and an *s*, like this:

    Delores + 's = Delores's

Delores's new car was hit in the parking lot.

bus + 's = bus's

The bus's brakes jammed, causing a minor accident.

b. If the noun is plural, add an apostrophe, like this:

shoes + ' = shoes'

All the shoes' laces are too long.

mayors + ' = mayors'

The three mayors' mutual aid agreement will yield economic benefits.

USE A COMPUTER

If you use your computer's spell check, remember that many programs do not check apostrophes in contractions, so misspellings such as "cant" will not be noted.

Narration

▶ THE PATTERN

Everyone likes a good story. We go to movies for good stories, we read books for good stories, and we gravitate toward people at parties who tell good stories. So taken are we by stories that we tell them to our children before they go to sleep. In writing, a story is called a narration, and this chapter will explain the techniques of effective narration.

▶ THE PURPOSES OF NARRATION

Obviously, a narration can entertain because a good story can amuse us and help us lose ourselves for a time. This fact helps explain the popularity of romance novels: they provide escapist entertainment. However, narrations can do more than entertain. For example, you can tell the story of the time you were cut from the basketball team if you want your reader to understand the lasting pain that experience caused you.

You can also tell a story to inform the reader of something. For example, you can tell the story of the time you were in a car accident if you want your reader to learn about the danger of sliding through a yellow light. Telling a story can also help you convince your reader to think or act a particular way. For example, to convince the reader that sexual harrassment is still a problem in the workplace, you can tell a story about a time you recently experienced or observed such harrassment.

A brief narration, called an *anecdote,* is often useful as a secondary pattern in other essays. For example, in an *exemplification* essay, an anecdote can be an example. If you want to illustrate that your mother is courageous, you can include a moving anecdote about the time she fended off an attack. A *comparison-contrast* that notes the differences between two mayoral candidates can include a telling anecdote about the time you met both candidates at a League of Women Voters meeting. A *cause-and-effect analysis* that explains the effects of current juvenile law can include a powerful anecdote from the newspaper about a young criminal who killed someone and was returned to the streets. A *process analysis* that explains how to surf can tell the story of the time you broke your leg because you failed to heed a caution you mention in the essay. Thus, while narration is often a pattern that stands alone, it also appears as an anecdote within other patterns of development.

Narration in College Writing

Narration can be a frequent component of college writing. For instance, a history paper on the events leading up to the Holocaust can tell the story of "The Night of the Broken Glass," when Jewish homes and businesses were looted and destroyed. A political science paper can narrate an account of the events following the Watergate break-in. Narrations are also frequently required in writing courses when students are asked to relate their personal experiences and in journalism classes when students are asked to write newspaper-style accounts of current events or campus happenings.

Narration is particularly useful for illustrating a point. Thus, if you write a paper for an education class and argue that people with learning disabilities do not get appropriate support in the classroom, you might tell the story of the time a learning-disabled friend was ignored in a high school algebra class. In a paper for a criminal justice class, you could support your point that judges should give out harsher penalties by telling the story of an offender who was repeatedly released, only to commit more crimes.

▶ SUPPORTING DETAILS

A narration usually includes the answers to the journalist's questions who, what, when, where, why, and how. That is, the story explains *who* was involved, *what* happened, *when* it happened, *where* it happened, *why* it happened, and *how* it happened. Of course, some answers may not be appropriate for some narrations, but they are a good starting point for generating ideas. Also, different answers may be emphasized in different narrations. Thus, in some stories *who* was involved may get a great deal of attention, but in other stories, *when* it happened may be more significant and thus treated with more detail.

In addition to the answers to the journalist's questions, narration often includes descriptive detail. When a person's appearance is important to the story, that person will be described; when locale is important, a place will be described.

To advance the story and add vividness, narrations often include conversation. To appreciate what conversation can add to a story, consider the difference between these two approaches:

1. Katie yelled to her mother and asked if she remembered to pick them up. Louise responded that she had, as she reached for the shoebox with the new tap shoes in it.
2. "Hi, Mom," Katie yelled. "Did you remember to pick them up?" "Yes, darlin'," Louise responded, reaching for the shoebox with the new tap shoes in it.

The second example is more vivid and interesting because of the use of conversation. (When you use conversation, be sure to check a handbook for correct capitalization and punctuation.)

If the reader needs additional information to appreciate the story, you can provide background information or an explanation of something. For example, if you tell a story about changing schools in tenth grade, you may want to explain why you changed schools and how you felt about your previous school.

Finally, since stories are often told because they make a particular point, a narration can include a statement of significance of the story. For example, in "Salvation" Langston Hughes tells a story about attending a revival service when he was 12. He concludes his narration with a statement of the story's significance, which reads, in part:

I didn't believe there was a Jesus any more, since he didn't come to help me.

▶ SELECTING AND ORDERING DETAILS

If you've ever listened to someone tell a story and drone on and on, you know how important it is to select narrative details carefully to avoid boring your reader with unnecessary information. This means you must choose carefully which *who, what, when, where, why,* and *how* questions to answer. It also means you must be careful not to include insignificant details, and you must not emphasize minor points, or your reader will grow annoyed. In other words, the key to a successful narration is pacing.

Arranging narrative details usually involves placing the events in chronological order. Most often this means beginning with the first event, moving to the second, on to the third, and so on. Variations of this pattern are possible, however. For some stories, you may want to begin at the end or in the middle, then flash back to the beginning.

Say, for example, you want to narrate an account of a car accident you were involved in. You could begin with the first event and move forward to the last event, like this:

> A year ago, I was on my way to pick up my girlfriend, looking forward to a pleasant dinner. As I approached the intersection at Fifth and Grove, the light turned yellow, but I figured I had plenty of time to slide through.

After this opening, you would narrate an account of the accident and then go on to tell about its aftermath.

You could also begin at the end and flash back to the beginning, like this:

> As I walked out of my last physical therapy session, I thought about how remarkable it is that I can walk at all. The accident nine months earlier had left me in critical condition with a smashed pelvis.

From here, you would flash back to the beginning and narrate an account of the accident and all the events up to the time you walked out of your last physical therapy session.

You could also begin in the middle of the chronology, like this:

> I remember waking up in the hospital with my parents and sister at my side. Mom was crying and Dad looked worried. In an instant the pain overwhelmed me and I could not remember what happened. Then all at once I remembered the accident.

From this point in the middle, you would flash back to the beginning and narrate an account of the accident. You would then move chronologically through the events until you reached the last event, walking out of your last physical therapy session.

To signal chronological order, move smoothly through your time sequence, and help your reader follow the events, you can use transitions like the following:

meanwhile	later	next
soon	at first	in the meantime
second	the next day	at the same time

If you want to explain something, do so at the point in the narration where the explanation is called for. If you want to state the point your narration makes, doing so in the conclusion or in the thesis can be effective.

Many times writers omit the introduction and thesis in a narration and begin instead with the first event in the story. However, if your reader needs background information to appreciate the story, the introduction is an excellent place to supply it. Your thesis can mention the story you will tell and the significance of that story, like this:

> When my younger brother and I got lost in the woods, I learned the real meaning of responsibility. (The story is about the time the writer got lost in the woods, and the significance is that the writer learned the meaning of responsibility.)

Because a story is told in chronological order, writers often omit topic sentences. The time sequence provides a clear structure, so the reader often does not need the organizational signposts provided by topic sentences.

Formal conclusions, too, may be omitted in narrations, particularly if the last event in the narration provides sufficient closure. However, if you want to state the significance of the story and you have not already done so, the conclusion can be an excellent spot for this information.

▶ SUGGESTIONS FOR WRITING NARRATION

1. Pick a story for a reason. Rather than just telling a story for the sake of telling a story, have a purpose in mind: to entertain your reader, to inform or persuade your audience of something, and/or to relate an experience to your audience. If you have a purpose in mind, your story will be more interesting because it will have a point.

2. To generate ideas, make a list with the answers to the *who, what, when, where, why,* and *how* questions. Decide which of these should be emphasized.

3. Identify important features about people and places and note them as points in the narration where you may want to add descriptive details.

4. Write out a statement of the significance of your narration.

5. Write your draft in one sitting; do not worry about anything except getting all the events down and answering all the appropriate journalist's questions.

Checklist for Revising Narration
1. Have you answered all the applicable journalist's questions? Are the appropriate answers emphasized?
2. Have you described people and scenes when these are important to the story?
3. Where appropriate, have you provided conversation to advance the narration and add vividness?
4. If the reader requires it, have you provided necessary background information?
5. Can your reader easily determine what point your narration makes?
6. Have you omitted extraneous details that slow the pace?
7. Are your details arranged in chronological order, with or without flashback?
8. Have you used transitions to help your reader follow the chronology?

The Family Reunion, Revisited

Robbie Warnick

Student writer Robbie Warnock shares an account of the annual family reunion and comes to see the event differently now than in the past. As you read, notice the important role description plays in this narration.

▼

1   Once a year, with the regularity of Old Faithful, scores of people claiming to be my kin would storm my hometown. The brood did not appear gradually, but as a veritable deluge of eccentricity, and often senility. The family's elders, in their twenty-year-old gas guzzlers, circled the town like vultures, finally "nesting" at the community center. As the rusty doors squeaked open in protest, I could almost hear John Williams's "Imperial March" blasting dirgelike through my mind. It was time for the annual family reunion, and I dreaded it as much as a trip to the dentist because to a youngster like me, everyone was as old as Methuselah and as quirky as Larry, Moe, and Curly.

2   Every woman present was clad in a floral spring dress, each with a distinct pattern. Most of the botanical togs reeked of mothballs. This pungent aroma was the only thing that held the bees attracted by the dress at bay. The men, on the other hand, looked like reject golfers or court jesters in their mismatched clothes of many colors. After each example of Henry Ford's worst nightmare had ejected the people crammed inside, the center's double doors were opened, and the celebration commenced.

3   Food is a major love for my family, which explains why portliness is the status quo. At the reunion, long wooden tables, like those in Hrothgar's meadhall, were laden with all types of dishes. However, an elderly matriarch of the clan became discontented with the same old food served every year. To ease the monotony, she created the "Annual Odd Recipe Contest," the goal of which was to create the most appetizing dish from the most bizarre ingredients.

4   I was present at the inception of this contest, albeit reluctantly. Along with the down-home staples, fried chicken and chocolate layer cake, I sampled a curious-looking green and purple casserole. Immediately, I fell victim to Aunt Frankie's infamous "Eggplant and Kudzu Surprise." Upon tasting the foul abomination, I fled to the nearest McDonald's and vowed never to consume another bite even remotely connected with the old crone.

Paragraphs 5 and 6
Details are in chronological order, and each paragraph begins with a transitional phrase. Details emphasize *who* and *what*. The vivid description continues.

5   After eating the wonderful meal of poultry and vegetation, the family would seek amusement. Refusing to simply converse the evening away, the motley crew would begin to square dance. Recovering from whatever odd recipe I had unwittingly subjected myself to, I would glance inside to view a plethora of octogenarians tramping and stomping in a futile attempt at dancing. Then the entertainment took a nosedive. Uncle Oliver produced a set of bagpipes and unleashed a sonic aberration akin to the sound produced when a few dozen cats are run over slowly by a bulldozer.

6   After the musical torture, the group underwent a schism. The men ditched their wives and each group would nestle in a separate corner and settle down enough to actually begin conversations unrelated to food. Now the talk focused on the past. At just the right moment, Uncle Oliver presented a hundred or so bags, each sealed, labeled, and containing a piece of debris from the family homeplace. As he presented these heirlooms, he recited a stentorian lecture on the "sacred domicile." Each member of the family then received a fragment of the house.

Paragraph 7
The conclusion presents the last event and the significance of the narration (the reunion served an important purpose). The last paragraph also answers *why*.

7   Stomach churning, ears smarting, and bearing a Ziploc bag containing a burnt bit of shingle, I returned home at the end of the day, praising God for deliverance. Today, I see things differently, however. Rather than eccentricity, I see love and a memorial to past times. The would-be Scotsman Oliver wanted the kids to cherish their heritage. I now regret my impatience and impudence because I realize that the reunion was an annual link between the past and the present. I now realize that the past is a treasure and the key to the future. For one more chance to remember and relive those times, I would square dance, listen to bagpipes, and even choke down kudzu.

My First Pair of Skates

I was fascinated by the bright and very colorful lights all around the skating rink. Back when I was thirteen years old and to this day, I feel that roller skating is the best thing that ever happened to me. When my family moved to Ohio, my new-found friends would go roller skating every weekend. I had to use rental skates because I didn't have my own. The rentals were brown, dingy, and very old compared to those of my friends who all had their own really cool skates. Their skates had wide wheels, a low cut boot, and good wheel bearings, which meant they were designed for speed. I couldn't keep up with my friends because of my rental skates. "It's not the skates that make the skater" is what all my friends would say to me. Maybe that's true, but a good pair sure would have helped. I couldn't go fast because I was stuck with cheap rentals.

Every weekend we would all go to Rocky's Skating Center. Upon entering, there was a display case that was very bright and eye-catching. The lights accented everything from skates to wheels, boots, basically everything I wanted. I always looked at all the cool new skates, wheels, and bearings; even the tools to fix skates were nice. I wanted everything in the case but was unable to have any of the contents. I was not a very good student, nor did I do any chores at home. I was very rebellious, so I didn't deserve anything in the display case. I would just stare and imagine what those skates would look like on my feet and how much better I would be able to skate if I had a pair.

A few weeks later, I was at the skating rink, just staring at the display case. There were a couple pairs of skates that I wanted, but they were way too expensive. One pair was $800; another pair was $350, but the pair I wanted was $199. The price was still a little high, but I knew I would take care of them if I had them. Getting my mother to buy them for me was my main concern. The skates were really nice with all-white boots, a blue plate, and blue wheels. I love the color blue, so I felt like it was my destiny to get this pair of skates. The skates were my size and my favorite color; everything was perfect except that they were not mine. I knew I would have to impress my mother somehow. A light bulb went off above my head. I had a great idea: my report card.

My first grading period was over, and I had received my report card in the mail. I got three C's, two B's, and one A. Of course, the A was in my gym class, but that is not the point. I worked very hard for those grades. Although they were not the highest, I did my best. I took the report card to my mother, and she said, "Well, I know you could have done better, but these are better than the last."

I said, "Mom, there's a pair of skates that I like. Since I go skating every weekend, could I have them? I know I could have done better, but please?"

"Yes, but it's going to be one of your Christmas presents," she told me.

I remember saying, "Thank you. You won't regret it."

The dream I had about having those blue and white skates finally came true. After that, skating was never the same. My skill level advanced quickly, and now my friends could barely keep up with me. It didn't matter if we were skating forwards or backwards, no one could catch me. I learned a few new tricks, like skating on my two front wheels and power sliding, which is a way to stop. Power sliding is the same way hockey players stop when they turn their blades against the ice, which sends shavings of ice away from them. This was useful when I was going really fast and a person cut me off. With this move, I could either stop quickly or enable myself to make a quick maneuver. Skating on your toes sounds easy, but it isn't. I skated on my toes until my feet would hurt and start to cramp up. This cramp was no ordinary painful cramp; it was a pain that I'd never felt before, but that didn't stop me from trying the move over and over again, no matter how bad it hurt because this trick opened up a lot more ability to integrate into moves such as the "iceberg," which is difficult. While I was on my toes and going backwards, I would lay my right skate on its inside top wheel. Then while I was in that position, I would do the same with my left skate. This was my favorite trick because it appeared that I was sliding sideways as if I were on ice. If I hadn't learned to skate on my toes, this trick would not have been possible.

I love roller skating; that's all there is to it. Ever since I was six, skating has been a part of my life. My sister Angel introduced me to roller skating even though she was only taking me to get out of babysitting. I enjoyed every minute of being at the skating rink. Still to this date, I skate 15 to 20 hours a week. Whenever I am sad, or I just need to get away, skating is my sanctuary. I am now 28 years old, and I currently work at Rocky's Skating Center. That first pair of skates is a reminder of how much skating means to me and how far I have come in the sport I love.

By Diego Avila

Instructor: Nora Wagner
Took Basic Writing: Fall 2010
Major: Nursing
Advice: "Don't be afraid to ask questions in class. And use the Writing Lab. It's a great tool to make your paper better and get advice from tutors. They always give you a good perspective."

Questions to Inspire Writing

1. Write about a memorable roller rink experience.
2. There is a display case at the roller rink full of attractive new skates that Diego covets. Write about a similar "window shopping" experience when you saw something you wanted a great deal. Did you get it? How?
3. Diego persuades his mother to buy him the roller skates when he gets an improved report card. Write about a time when you convinced a parent, older relative, teacher, or boss of something important.
4. Write about a time when you were rewarded for an improved report card or some other accomplishment.
5. What sport, activity, or hobby has long been an important part of your life?

6.   Diego excelled at skating and could do all kinds of tricks. In what sport or activity do you excel? Explain and describe.

7.   Diego is dissatisfied with the quality of the old rental skates he has to use, and his friends comfort him with "It's not the skates that make the skater." Write about a time when you felt limited because of inferior materials. If, like Diego, you were able to eventually upgrade, write about how the new and improved equipment did or did not make a difference. If you were not able to upgrade, how did that work out?

8.   What is the "best thing that ever happened to" you?

9.   What was the one thing you always "dreamed about" owning? What happened once you owned it?

10. What hobby or sport do you enjoy and why?

11. The roller rink is Diego's "sanctuary." What is your sanctuary?

12. Diego feels roller skating is the best thing that ever happened to him. What activity or sport was good for you?

13. Diego used his good grades as a way to influence his mom to buy the skates. What have you done to get a parent to buy you something or do something for you?

14. What was going through your mind when you read this?

Building On a Rocky Foundation

Last year was my first year coaching at a local Akron high school, and it started out as my living hell. My brother, David, applied for the job when he found an ad in the newspaper. He got the job and asked me to be his assistant coach saying, "You understand young girls better than I do." In hindsight, I might disagree with this statement. I walked into our first practice with 32 girls and one boy. I had met only half the team, and the other half were nameless and faceless to me. To be honest, aside from the boy, when they are all wearing white t-shirts, black shorts, and pony tails, they all looked alike. Out of 100 cheerleaders, here were the 33 chosen. I'd known their skills, but that was it. I was extremely intimidated because my experiences with cheerleaders, even though I had been one, weren't always tasteful. I was also intimidated because this was my first time coaching any sport and oddly enough, I wasn't more than three years older than most of the seniors.

Now as a coach, it is very important to treat all the girls as equals, regardless of whom you like or dislike. I knew this was important, but I couldn't help liking some of the girls a lot and others less. I assure you, I would never make it apparent among the girls who were on my dislike list. It was simply a topic talked about between coaches in confidence. Within my first week, I had my favorites and my least favorites. One of my least favorites was a very talented senior, Maddy. She was a great game-day cheerleader and an awesome base spot, but she had more attitude than the whole team combined. She second guessed my drills, requirements, and logic at all times. Even things as simple as what color briefs to wear underneath their skirts became an argument. I started by refusing to argue and repeating myself, "Please do not talk back. Just do as I ask of you." I repeated and repeated this for about two weeks before my frustration grew. Her responses were normally, "What did I do now?" or "I'm not being disrespectful." Maddy always had to have the last word, topped with an eye roll or a huff. My next step was to condition her individually until she was too tired to talk back. This worked for awhile, but soon I think she started to pick up on my antics. She was just getting stronger while conditioning and soon was able to still mouth off while doing pushups. Finally, one day I cracked. To be totally honest, I don't remember what exactly she said, but I remember being at my wits' end. I couldn't take the attitude she had, and I was worried it would rub off onto the rest of the squad. I needed a solution before I lost the respect of the rest of the team as well. I had this extreme idea. They were a team, and when one individual was trouble, the whole team would reap the consequences. I didn't want to be cruel, but I was forced to punish the team as a whole. In my past experiences, the slacker would be pressured by the rest of the team to pick up the pace. Little did I know, Maddy would be much more stubborn than I expected.

After about three months, the conditioning was getting to be redundant. I would bet that my cheerleading squad did more push-ups than the football team that season. The team was so talented, but they were misguided by their upperclassman. I hoped to find leadership in some of the juniors because punishing Maddy alone didn't help. Her attitude only got much worse. I was hoping to encourage the younger girls to stand up to her as a team, but the younger girls were just intimidated by her.

The coaches before my brother and me were immature and downright mean. The school had been through six cheerleading coaches in two years. Maddy had pretty much taken over the squad until we came in. As a whole, the squad didn't trust us, and sadly, I couldn't blame them for it. Their old coaches were not responsible and often times left them unattended at practices and games. When they were present, they often would curse in front of the girls and say inappropriate things. They openly picked favorites and would pressure the girls to do skills they were scared of in threatening ways. Cheerleading often gets the reputation of being a sissy sport, but I can assure you it's not by any means. Cheerleading consists of gymnastics, dance, and acrobatics. It often can be dangerous if the proper steps are not applied in progression. The coaches before my brother and me were not conscientious about this at all. They would force the girls to try new tumbling tricks without proper training and weren't concerned with injuries. When the girls were injured or sore, the coaches often yelled, "Suck it up!" Clearly, their previous coaches were not beneficial role models.

After a very shaky football season and many, many tears shed by both the girls during practice and me after practice, it was time to take on the competition season. The competition season was always my favorite because it showcased the cheerleaders alone. The competition side of cheerleading is more about skill level rather than just cheer or dance. With cheerleading mats, the team is allowed by the Ohio High School Athletic Association to perform to their full ability rather than the rules enforced during football or basketball season. The mats are more giving to falls, and in turn, the rules allow high school cheerleading teams to do bigger, harder, and faster tricks. I was very apprehensive about another season with my trouble maker, Maddy. Even though Maddy often had a bad attitude, the team needed her skill level.

In only the first week of competition practices, it was apparent our team was going to have a very good routine. We would definitely have a chance at winning states. Oddly enough, Maddy seemed to have gone through a complete transformation. She was determined to get new skills. She encouraged the team to strive for her accomplishments. My brother and I just couldn't get our hopes up, so I kept waiting for the attitude to come back out. One day while running the routine during practice, she called out, "Let's go, girls! Come on!" My brother and I shared a look of awe. I was truly stunned she was being a positive influence on the team. The more progress we made, the better Maddy's attitude got. She was excited for practice and came ready to work. She encouraged the girls to try harder and stepped up into a leadership role. It not only shocked me, but other coaches, teachers and her parents showed a very surprised expression. The harder she worked, the better our team got. Maddy was successful, and the team seemed to feel the way we were coming together. The more she was challenged with new skills, the better she performed. It was only a matter of time before Maddy and I shared jokes and talked after practice. She seemed to respect and trust me. That year my team went to states and placed second. Although we would have preferred first, hitting our routine was a better accomplishment.

I suppose Maddy taught me a valuable lesson. Coaching is not easy, and it's not something that can be taught. Coaching styles are all different, and none are necessarily wrong. Once I gained confidence in myself and my team, the pieces fell into place. Maddy taught me that strong bonds can be built on rocky and uneven foundations.

By Erin Colopy

Instructor: Dr. Michelle Miller
Took Basic Writing: Spring 2010
Major: Art Education
Advice: "Definitely read from your class textbooks." They were "helpful in writing papers."

Questions to Inspire Writing

1. Write about a new job that intimidated you at first. Describe the job and emphasize the parts of it that were especially intimidating.

2. Like Erin, sometimes young people have to supervise others only a bit younger than they are (or even the same age or older). Write about a time when you faced this sort of challenge.

3. Write about a time when you were (or weren't) treated equally or fairly by a coach, teacher or boss, or write about a time when you had to face a challenge of treating those who worked for you fairly.

4. Erin, the coach, and Maddy, the senior cheerleader, were engaged in a power struggle. Write about someone with whom you had an extended power struggle.

5. Write about this line: "When one individual was trouble, the whole team would reap the consequences." Write about a time when you were punished as a part of a group for something one person (or a few) did.

6. Erin works to find a way to get along with Maddy. Describe the strategies you took to deal with a "problem" person in your life.

7. Maddy not only intimidated the younger cheerleaders, she also intimidated the previous cheerleading coaches. Write about a person you know with the power to intimidate.

8. Erin asserts that cheerleading is a sport and seeks to prove that point by discussing the grueling practices and their competitions. Were you involved with cheerleading? How was it a sport? Did you try to convince others of this? How?

9. What was your "living hell?" Did it remain that way?

10. Erin describes the cheerleading squad before she and her brother took it over as one where mistrust poisoned the atmosphere. Write about an experience in your life where mistrust polluted a potentially good environment.

11. Write about someone you know, perhaps yourself, who has or had "attitude."

12. Have you ever changed your opinion of someone? Who? Why?

13. Tell about a memorable experience when you were coached.

14. Erin's relationship with Maddy is very rocky at the start, but they grow to respect and like each other. Describe a relationship you had with someone that changed for the better or worse over time.

15. Erin coached a cheerleading squad. Have you ever coached? What was that like?

16. Maddy is someone who in the end rises to a challenge. Write about someone (including yourself) who did or didn't rise to a challenge.

17. What was going through your mind when you read this?

My Scar

The nurse walks into my room and says, "It's time." She unlocks the wheels on my bed and unplugs my IV unit from the wall. I'm rolled out of the room and begin the journey. I look up and watch the lights on the ceiling repeat over and over. They create a flashing strobe light effect. The nurse is rushing me down the long halls. A sharp pain comes from the port in my hand. The nurse doesn't realize she's tugging too hard on my IV unit. We finally arrive at the waiting room. My parents, looking around nervously, smile when they see me arrive. We wait for the uncertainty ahead. I have a huge pit in my stomach, and soon fear falls over my body. Another nurse comes in, bringing with her something to calm my nerves and relax my body. It's amazing laughing gas. I inhale the fruity strawberry scent, and within minutes I am laughing up a storm. Never clearly aware of what I am giggling at, I have a steady stream of tears coming from my eyes. I kiss my mommy and daddy goodbye. A nurse pushes me through two giant doors. I enter an all-white room, bright as the sun. The lights are everywhere. There is an especially huge light anchored above me. I glance around and see several nurses and doctors in blue scrubs. A friendly anesthesiologist, who approaches me suddenly, attaches a syringe to my port. It is full of a white substance called sodium pentothal. She slowly injects the medicine and asks me to count back from ten. I begin ten, nine, eight.... I saw my gown fly over my face. I never made it to seven. I was in a deeper sleep than a bear during hibernation; the cutting had begun.

I live with Idiopathic Thrombocytopenic Purpura, or simply put ITP. ITP is a bleeding disorder. The immune system attacks and destroys the platelets. Platelets are necessary for blood to clot normally, but a body that is infected with the disease has very few of them. The attack starts when the immune system produces antibodies against the platelets. The spleen senses them as harmful and destroys the platelets carrying the antibodies. The cause is still unknown, and a prevention method has not been discovered yet.

At the young age of two, I began developing symptoms. The slightest bump or touch on my body would create the most large, painful, colorful bruise. My parents, unaware of how I was developing bruises all over, knew something was wrong and made an appointment with the doctor. Something was visibly wrong. I was immediately given a vast array of tests. First was a check for cancers. The specialist thought leukemia could have been the source of my symptoms. The result was negative. I was tested for several disorders that suited my condition. They resulted in the same negative answer. The decision was made to also withdraw bone marrow from my back and hips in search for some answers. Everything seemed hopeless. A couple years passed by during the time of testing as we waited for a diagnosis to come to light. When I was five, the choice was made to take me to the University of Florida, where years of searching finally came to an end. The discovery of my condition was made. There was a relief in knowing help could be provided now.

The doctors warned my family of my condition, and I required twenty-four hour attention. Due to the lack of care my spleen was having for my platelets, trips, falls, and hits to the head could possibly end my life. Soon after, this almost came true. I was carelessly playing one night and hit my head on the wall. I developed a baseball-sized lump on my head. My mother immediately called the paramedics, and I was rushed to the emergency room. I slightly remember events from that night. I can still see my mom's face painted in fear and the extremely bright blue and red lights filling the sky with color. I recovered, but after the accident, I went to a specialist and was fitted for a helmet to protect my head from falls. Due to the ITP, my brain could hemorrhage and cause me to have a stroke and become paralyzed on my right side of the body. As silly as the helmet sounded, I had to wear it.

Soon after the discovery of my disease, I turned six and entered the first grade. I was placed on the medicines that were known to cure the disease. They all began to work but only for a short time. I was left in the same ill state as before. The doctors looked into the last option for the answer: a splenectomy. My parents and doctors met, reviewing the procedures and possible complications of removing my spleen. They stated that I was a life risk patient. I was given a fifty-fifty chance of survival because my blood might not clot after the surgery; consequently, I could bleed to death. The doctors still encouraged my parents to move forward with the operation, and a date was set for my surgery. God was now about to role play through the doctor's hands and sew me a new life.

In exchange for my spleen, I was given a four-and-a-half inch scar on the top part of my stomach. I'm not very fond of the appearance of my mark, and the scar tissue causes sharp pains from time to time. I get asked questions when swimsuit season comes or when I'm changing clothes. I quickly explain that I had my spleen removed and continue with the task I am performing. I am thankful for my life, but sometimes I don't always show that. The limits to living life continue to haunt me to this day. I have to use caution when flying because of germs and illnesses, and high degree temperatures require me to report to the ER. Although I get upset from the physical appearance of the scar, I have grown and am inspired to see what a gift life can be. With this second chance, I strive to be the best and stay positive with every situation. The doctors may have taken my spleen, but they gave me life again and a whole new meaning with it.

By Amy Force

Instructor: Nora Wagner
Took Basic Writing: Fall 2010
Major: Nursing

Questions to Inspire Writing

1. Do you have a hospital or emergency room memory?
2. Do you have any scars? How did you "earn" them?

3. Amy writes about her pre-diagnosis symptoms and testing by doctors like it is a mystery to be solved. Write about mysterious symptoms you or a loved one had and how a diagnosis was (or wasn't) discovered.

4. Write about a time you saw someone's "face painted in fear."

5. Amy writes about limitations forced upon her by her condition, such as the need for caution when flying. What limitations do you or a loved one have to consider with respect to a health issue? How do you deal with these, practically and emotionally? Has how you have dealt with these limitations changed with time?

6. Amy concludes, "The doctors may have taken my spleen but gave me life again and a whole new meaning with it." Rewrite that from your point of view, filling in these blanks: "The _____ may have taken my _____, but it gave me _____."

7. Amy's scar is a constant reminder of her past and inspires her to appreciate life. What physical aspect of your body serves as a reminder to you?

8. What was going through your mind when you read this?

My Father: Mean, Heartless or Just Misunderstood?

Looking back to my childhood, I can remember a time when I was about four years of age and my father, David, was in the bathroom. He was shaving, and he had smeared shaving cream all over my face; my mother, Martha, just laughed and then proceeded to clean me up. That is a good memory that I can recall, but as I grew older and entered middle school, my father and I grew further apart. He didn't really do many activities with me after that. We didn't play games or play outside much at all. I guess he didn't have the patience or time to do things like tossing the softball around or playing with the Frisbee.

One thing I can always remember about my father was that I never received any praise from him when I received a good grade on my papers or report card from school. My mother, of course, was always there to tell me "Good job; I'm proud of you." It was nice to hear that from her, but the person I really wanted to hear it from never said those things. The things I heard from my father were "Do your homework," "Feed the animals," and "Mow the lawn."

I thought my father was a tyrant and that he received enjoyment out of barking orders or punishing my older brother Richard and me. I used to think the only attention I could receive from him was negative. I gave up on school and started failing or just barely receiving passing grades; then, I would get some attention from him. The paddling and groundings went on most of my time in middle school and junior high as a result of my grades. Finally, when I started high school, I pulled myself together and said to myself, it doesn't matter if I get praise from him or not; I'm going to pass my classes and graduate. After being held back twice and going to summer school, I graduated and received my diploma. I received no reaction whatsoever from my father. I then went out into the working world.

The working world was tough, but I did it, and I actually began to have a social life. My friends and I would go out bowling, playing pool, or to the night clubs. My father was there again, telling me things like, "You don't have time to be hanging out with your friends," and "Come home, do your chores, and go to work." I was 19 years of age when I first stood up to my father. I was angry and upset

that even though I was an adult, he was still treating me like a child. One day he had been nagging me

about wasting time with my friends. I told him, "I'm not a child anymore, Dad, so quit treating me like

one." He just looked at me strangely and said "Okay."

I still had restrictions, though, since I was still living in their house. I had to be in by midnight,

and if I was going to be late, I had to call. This went on for about five years; then, the real trouble

started. My father had been diagnosed with Lou Gehrig's disease. This made things even more difficult.

As stated on http:/www.answers.com, "Lou Gehrig's is a fatal neuron degenerative disease of the brain

and the spinal cord which in turn causes loss of muscle control and eventually death." On December 14,

1998, my father lost his two-year fight with the disease. That night was even more painful for me

because my father and I had argued about my coming home late again earlier that night, and he passed

away without my having a chance to make amends.

The years after that were hard for me. I was quick to anger and easy to provoke, and my brother

was no help because he was hurting as much as I was. He would treat me just like my father, and I would

yell at him, "You're not my father, so stop acting like him." After several fights, one day my mother

asked me why I was so angry, and I told her because of how Dad passed away and I was unable to make

peace with him. I asked my mother, "Why do I feel this way?" I had hated him for everything he put me

through, my never getting praise for good school work, and his never saying he was proud of me at all.

My mother told me these exact words, "Your father never got praise himself; your grandfather

was a very cold person. Your dad never graduated high school, but he did care about you and your

brother, and even though he didn't show it, he was proud of you and loved you. He was just trying to

teach you to be a man."

In closing, I can see now, years later, what my mother meant about what my father was trying to

do. I now know that my father was not a tyrant, just a father trying to do a better job than his did. I miss my father sometimes, but I know he's here watching over us, not mean, not heartless, just misunderstood.

By Randy Gallagher

Instructor: Dr. Michelle Miller
Took Basic Writing: Spring 2010
Major: Web Design and Development
Advice: "Write from the heart and the soul. Don't be afraid to let your feelings and emotions come out in your work."

Questions to Inspire Writing

1.   Randy begins by telling a sweet, happy childhood memory he has of his father. Write about an early memory of a parent, grandparent, or other relative.

2.   Relationships with fathers are different from relationships with mothers, and today, often harder to come by. Write about your relationship with your father.

3.   Randy's father only gives him negative comments and never praises him. Write about criticism or praise an older relative gave you. Or write about your overall experience of criticism and or praise from an older relative, teacher, or boss.

4.   There is a book and TV show called "$#*! My Dad Says," and Randy also quotes several things his father said. Make a list of things a person important in your life (like a parent, other relative, coach, teacher, etc.) said to you, and try to make meaning of what was said. Does it all fit one theme, or is there a mixed message? What wisdom might you take, and what might you discard from these messages?

5.   Randy writes about his father's struggle with Lou Gehrig's disease. Write about a time when you and your family had to cope with a family member's serious medical condition.

6.   Randy is hurt by the fact that since he and his father argued right before his father died, they did not have "a chance to make amends." Write about a lack of closure you have with someone important to you. Or, if you were able to make amends, write about that. How is it important to have this chance?

7. As a child, Randy thinks of his father as heartless; later, he realizes things about his father that help him to better understand and even appreciate him. Think about someone important in your life about whom you had very different views at different times.

8. When someone in a family dies or leaves, the dynamics and relationships change; Randy felt resentful that his older brother was trying to take their father's place. Write about a change in a family (or job or team) dynamics when someone was suddenly absent and the changing roles of the people.

9. Randy's mother gives him some perspective about father based upon his childhood, which Randy had never realized before. That helped him understand his father and his behavior more. Write about some information you found out later about someone important in your life that helped you better understand that person.

10. What did you do to gain the attention of a parent?

11. What was going through your mind when you read this?

What Scares Me the Most

If someone were to ask me what scares me the most at different times throughout my life, I suppose the response would never be the same. You see, as I grew up, my fears grew with me, and most of the things that used to scare me as a child I can now laugh at as an adult. I used to be afraid of something grabbing my feet from under the bed. I would run and leap into my bed at night with a starting distance of at least three feet. I watched too many scary movies at a young age. The memory of that makes me smile now.

My first memories of really being scared of anything, though, are of being alone. I was about two-years-old, and my older brother, Brion, then five, was left to watch me. I didn't even realize at first that my mother had left. I only remember being scared because she didn't come when I cried, and I think that was what really scared me. I used to be angry about that, but I now realize how naïve she was; I guess she didn't realize the danger we were in at the time.

My more recent memories of being afraid are of bugs. I wasn't always afraid of bugs. My older brother used to take me bug hunting and "garter snake" hunting with him. It was fun at first; we would go to the field or to the railroad tracks, which were about half a mile from our house. We would look under rocks, hunting for the tiny snakes escaping from the hot sun. We'd skim the shallow stream looking for crayfish. We hunted grasshoppers like we were on a safari, sneaking up on them through the tall grass as if they were wild beasts. After we caught our "pets for the day," we'd put them in a pickle jar or a coffee can with random sticks, leaves, and dirt, assuming we had recreated the poor captive animals' habitats. We tried to talk Mom into letting us keep them as pets, but of course the answer was always no. I loved getting to play with the bugs and make little homes for them. I sometimes would even give them names.

It was all fine until he got sick of me tagging along and wised up as to how to get rid of me. I used to hold and help catch the bugs: ants, crickets, spiders, snakes (which are actually reptiles), and the ultimate praying mantis, which was the mother of all things creepy. And of course, him being a nine-year-old little boy, he tried to have "matches," and made the bugs fight in a jar whenever possible. It was usually disappointing though as most bugs refused the barbaric act. Looking back, it was quite unethical, but at six years old, it seemed perfectly all right to me.

Then the day came when he no longer wanted his dirty-faced baby sister slowing him down. I guess maybe it wasn't cool anymore to be caught playing with his little "sissy." He decided it would be funny to tell me how "dangerous" the bugs we were handling actually were, knowing that once this information sank into my little brain, handling bugs would no longer appeal to me, freeing him of the tagalong burden that I was. He was actually a great storyteller for such a little boy. He told me about ants that eat human flesh, earwigs that crawl in your ears and eat your brain, spiders that kill you instantly when they bite, killer bees, diseases that kill you or make your hands fall off from the "bug germs," praying mantises that could cut your fingers off with their pinchers, and yes, grasshoppers that really did spit chewing tobacco in your hand (gross!).

At first, I didn't believe him. "Nuh-uh!" I shrieked, assuming he was just trying to trick me as he often did that just for laughs. I was gullible. But he remained serious and stone-faced. Then I figured, who was I to argue? He was much older and wiser than I was in his nine years, and he obviously knew what he was talking about. I was only six. As soon as he smelled the fear, he acted, and it was perfectly timed, come to think of it.

He slowly pulled a previously caught five-inch praying mantis out of the Maxwell House can and held it up high for me to see. I stared closely at it. I had never quite noticed how ugly they were before that moment. Its long arms with the serrated-like claws slowly motioned like a boxer waiting to throw the first punch. Its long pale green body seemed much larger now than it did earlier when it was just a cute little harmless bug in a coffee can. Its eyes were alien-like, and its tiny black pupils shifted quickly with any nearby motion. Its antennae were waving in a constant rhythm, almost as if dancing to a strange beat I couldn't hear. And suddenly the awful thing repulsed me, and that's when he asked me if I wanted to hold it. Did I want to hold it? That nasty thing? "Eww!, No!" I squealed, taking a step backwards and wrinkling my face up in sheer disgust.

He smiled, a slow Grinch-like smile, and took a step forward. He was enjoying this moment of power he had. He took another step towards me, and it became unspoken yet equally understood by both of us what was about to happen next. He giggled, and my eyes grew wide as I shook my head in denial. "Oh crap!"

As if a whistle had blown, we were both off racing towards the house, me running for my dear life, and him laughing hysterically at my sudden terror, holding out the offensive bug in front of him. It seemed to be a mile to our house, yet it was actually less than a block. Fortunately, for the sake of my poor dear life, I made it to the house before he did and "ratted" him out to my mom. He then got yelled at, and to my disappointment, was sent back outside. It must have been a hilarious sight to see, me running, waving my arms, screaming, and him chasing me, laughing uncontrollably. But I was traumatized.

Needless to say, his ingenious plan worked, and he no longer had to worry about me tagging along. I was no longer the sissy girl, ruining his snakes, snails, and puppy-dog tail days. And I no longer had any interest in any insect or reptile. I now considered creepy crawling things disgusting, and something I needed to avoid at all costs.

Today, I am no longer afraid to be alone. I actually seek alone time whenever possible. I find it hard to get with the way my life is today; privacy in a small house can be a real challenge sometimes. I like the quiet, reflective moments to just relax and think or read. My private moments come too few and far between, but when they do happen, they are savored.

As for bugs, I now have a phobia. I cannot stand the very thought of anything crawling on me. I can't even look closely at a bug without getting goose bumps and my hair standing on end. I really get so upset that it's embarrassing. I sometimes feel like I'm having an anxiety attack if a bug is too close to me.

And if a wasp or bee gets in the car while I'm driving, I will pull over and exit the vehicle until the hijacking insect flies out on its own.

All of the above is true, and there were more times like the ones mentioned that followed. Sometimes we can look back and laugh at what we are or have been afraid of throughout our lives, but some fears stay with us, whether we want them to or not. We can outgrow or manage a lot of our fears, and some fears we have are actually instinctive or beneficial. We have survival instincts to defend ourselves, or fear of death to enhance a will to live; sink or swim is another example of instinctive fear that can be beneficial. Others, like my fear of bugs, are useless, and can be quite annoying at a picnic.

By Leslie Habas

Instructor: Becky McDonald
Took Basic Writing: Fall 2010
Major: Undecided
Advice: "It's never too late."

Questions to Inspire Writing

1. Leslie developed a phobia about bugs. What scares you the most? Why do you have that fear?

2. Leslie writes, "As I grew up, my fears grew with me." How did your fears change over the course of your life?

3. Leslie says she watched too many scary movies as a small child. Were you ever influenced by a scary movie?

4. Leslie's brother tells her outlandish tales of the danger of insects. Write about family members or friends who told you similar lies for sport. How did that work out?

5. When he is a little older, Leslie's brother "no longer wanted his dirty-faced baby sister slowing him down." Write about a time when an older sibling left you behind for a time or a time when you, as the older sibling, tried to escape a younger sibling.

6. Leslie's brother enjoys a moment of power. Write about a moment of power you enjoyed or a moment of someone else's power that you endured.

7. Leslie acknowledges that she was very gullible when it came to believing stories her brother told. Who in your family (or among friends) is or was the story teller? What's the most memorable story? How were you affected by that?

8. What was going through your mind when you read this?

The Best and the Worst 4 x 100 Relay

Junior high was an exciting time in my life. There were so many different and new extracurricular activities to choose from. The most exciting for me was sports. I had always enjoyed playing various sports as a child, and I was excited about all of the different sports that junior high had to offer. There were so many I could have chosen, but cross country is the one that caught my interest. I was not entirely sure what cross country was at the time, but I decided I would give it a try. The first day of practice is when I fell in love with running. I may not have understood my newfound obsession at first, but I knew that I could not stay away from it. Unfortunately, the cross country season seemed to be a short one, and soon I found myself in desperate need of an excuse to run. Luckily, track practice started a few months later and soon became my favorite sport. By eighth grade, I had my events down and was very good at them. My coach had started me on hurdles and I loved them. From then on, that is the event I focused on in track until the last meet of my eighth grade year. It was at that meet that I learned how important it is to cope with the situations you are thrown into and also that nothing is a complete failure as long as you really tried your best.

My eighth grade year, we made it to the Pac-7 championships. There was so much tension on the bus ride to Tuslaw High School that you could have cut it with a knife. The team really had nothing to worry about since we had gone undefeated all season. Most of us thought that this was going to be a cake walk, and we would walk away with the Pac-7 trophy. When we got there, it was overcast, and the sun was just starting to rise. I can still remember the cool crisp feeling of the morning air in my lungs as I stood there on the edge of the track field. We all could smell the sweet scent of victory in the air. The field events were going to start first, so everyone in those events began to congregate for warm ups and stretches. My first event was the 110 meter high hurdles, which would not begin until later in the morning. I have to admit that I was feeling a little nervous despite the fact that I had, at some point, beaten everyone I would be running against that day. Time passed slowly, but eventually it was time for my first event. The starter told us to get to our marks, get set, and then the gun went off loudly. It was over before I knew it. I placed first a whole second ahead of everyone else. Afterward, I headed up to the stands to relax until my next race, which would be the 300 meter low hurdles. I enjoyed watching my teammates compete in their own events while I waited to run again.

The sun was so nice and warm that I decided to take a little nap. I pulled my hat down over my eyes and put my head back. I had just started to doze off when I was abruptly awakened by something that sounded like a dying cow. I quickly looked to see my coach running around, shouting for someone, but I could not quite hear what he was saying. He reminded me of that carnival game where you shoot the duck and it turns around and goes the other way. He would run over and ask someone if they had seen the person; then, one of the teammates would shoot him, and he would turn and run the other way. He did this for about five minutes, and then someone pointed toward the stands, and "ding," he started toward the stands. When he finally reached the crowded stands, I could see how desperately he needed to find whoever he was looking for. His frantic eyes bounced from person to person sitting there until they met mine. A look of relief came over his face as he yelled for me to join him.

We started down toward the track, and I kept asking him what was going on; he seemed to not hear me. After our brisk walk, I stopped and said I was not going any further until he told me what was going on. He told me that Justin sprained his ankle and would not be able to run the 4 x 100 meter relay. We had a back up, but he was already running three events, and in junior high, that is all they allow you to run. I was the fastest person not running three events, so I was now the back up. The running I had no problem with. It was the passing of the baton that I was worried about, as well as the fact that I had never run that particular race before. The coach kept telling me that I would do fine, but I really think he was trying to reassure himself more than me.

I do not think I had a choice in the matter, but I told him that I would do it. I went over to the rest of the 4 x 100 team, and we started to practice handing off the baton. We were still dropping the baton after twenty minutes of practice, but we were out of time as the starter called for all of the 4 x 1 teams. The starter went through how the race was going to work and where we were supposed to line up. The team's faces were white as if we had all just seen how we were going to die. We went to our starting points. I did not notice how many people were in the stands at first, but as I walked in front of them, I started to get a lump in my throat. I could feel the sweat pouring down my forehead, and it was not from the scorching sun. I tried to block the loud, obnoxious, screaming fans out of my mind but could not.

With a startling blast, the race started. My mind was running faster than the people actually running the race. Brad started the race off because he was the fastest out of the blocks. He got to the first hand off and flawlessly passed John the baton. John was fast, but most people could beat him in a 100 meter race. He was the second leg because people could not muscle him out of the way when they broke in. Steven was the third leg, and now that he had the baton, it was about to be my turn. My heart was thumping as fast as a hummingbird's. He was at the tennis ball, and that meant that it was time for me to get going. I started running and put my hand back to get the baton. As soon as I felt the cold metal hit my skin, I took off at full speed. I wanted to win so badly, but I could see the Tuslaw runner coming up beside me. The finish was right there in front of me. I put my head down and ran through the line. After the last runner crossed the line, we had to wait for the results because the finish was too close; no one knew who had won. The coach came running over to us with a smile from ear to ear. As we tried to catch our breath, someone finally asked if we had won. He told us that he did not care if we won or not. To be able to come together like that and have a chance to win was all that mattered.

There has not been a day since that race in junior high where I have experienced such a wide range of emotions. I was excited, terrified, humbled, and proud. My teammates and I were thrown together unexpectedly, and yet we were able to find a way to work together and come out on top. We may not have won the 4 x 1 relay that day, but we still won the Pac-7 trophy. I remember wanting to find a dark corner to hide in when my coach told me that I was running the race, but now, looking back at the situation, I would not change a thing about the way the events of that day played out. I learned from that day that if I put my mind to something, I can usually accomplish it. More importantly, I learned the importance of trying my best, no matter the situation I am in or the expected outcome.

By Ryan Holland

Instructor: Paula Miller
Took Basic Writing: Spring 2010
Major: Automated Manufacturing Engineering
Advice: Some of what is done in class "seems redundant and unimportant now, but it will really help you in your classes."

Questions to Inspire Writing

1. Ryan "fell in love" with running. Write about a sport or extracurricular activity that you fell in love with in your school days.

2. While Ryan is relaxing after a race, his coach drafts him to run in a relay as a substitute. Write about a time when you were called upon at the last minute to fill in for somebody else and how it worked out.

3. Ryan says that before the race, the coach was trying to reassure himself as much or more than Ryan. Write about a time when someone tried to convince you of something (or when you tried to convince someone else), and it seemed like the person talking was trying to convince him- or herself.

4. Ryan goes into slow-motion detail of the race itself. Describe in similar detail an event where you competed.

5. Ryan writes that the coach "told us that he did not care if we won or not. To be able to come together like that and have a chance to win was all that mattered." Write about a time (athletic or otherwise) when there was something more important than winning and people united for a cause.

6. Ryan writes about the wide range of emotions he felt in this experience. Write about a memorable experience where you too felt many (sometimes conflicting) emotions.

7. When he is first called from the stands by his coach to run this race, Ryan writes that he wanted to "hide in a corner," but he later was thrilled to have had this experience. Write about a time when your reluctance to do something was later overwhelmed by your happiness at having had the opportunity.

8. Describe a time you were thrown into an unexpected situation. What were the circumstances? How did you do?

9. What was going through your mind when you read this?

Top Thrill Dragster

It was August, 2, 2009, my one year wedding anniversary of being married to the love of my life. My husband and I didn't have a honeymoon the year before. It was a warm, beautiful, Sunday morning, and we were headed to Cedar Point, the amusement park in Sandusky, Ohio.

The night before leaving, we made sure to stop at the grocery store to purchase a few snacks and drinks to take with us; we knew the food at the amusement park would be expensive. We finally got on the road and on our way to Cedar Point. We made sure to leave early in the morning to avoid traffic and to avoid the long lines that were sure to be ahead of us. I tried to fall asleep on the way up there, but I was too excited to be going; I hadn't been to an amusement park since my senior year of high school, which was in 2005. I made my husband drive.

Finally, arriving at Cedar Point a little after 10 a.m. when they opened, I was amped and ready to ride every ride there was in the park. I remember the last time I was at Cedar Point, there was one ride I was too chicken to ride on, and so I vowed that I would go on it this time around. Entering the amusement park, my husband looked up and pointed and said, "That's what we're riding first!" I looked in the direction of his finger, and sure enough it was pointing at the ride that I was too chicken to get on the last time, the Top Thrill Dragster.

This ride is a very simple ride; it goes up a hill and down a hill, and that's it. Sounds pretty boring, but this was no ordinary ride. It reaches 120 miles per hour in less than 4 seconds as it climbs a 420 foot hill, slightly turning at a 90 degree angle, and comes spiraling down at 270 degrees, then to the finish line. This ride is only a 17 second ride. When I realized that he was talking about the Dragster, my heart skipped a beat, literally. I was begging and pleading with my husband to let it be that last ride of the day. I was scared out of my pants, and I wanted to ride something a little less extreme so early in the morning. My husband, Ahmad, dragged me to the ride's Finish Line.

Before you enter any ride, they give you safety tips of do's and don'ts for that specific ride. The first thing I remember reading was, "If you have a heart problem, do not ride." My heart was ready to jump out of my chest as I read this warning. At that time, I felt as if I had a heart problem and was ready to get out of the line just as soon as I got in the line, Ahmad still dragging me through the metal bars to where the line stood. The line wasn't long at all, so we were able to pass through the metal bars that break the line up pretty fast. I started psyching myself up, telling myself, "It's going to be okay; you have ridden so many roller coasters, it will be a piece of cake." I then lost my fear for a slight second or two, and then I saw one of the cars to the ride take off, and just as soon as it took off, it was right back down. From where we were standing in the line, I could see the passengers' faces; it looked as if they all had swallowed their hearts and spit them back up into their chests. I was terrified once again and now ready to urinate on myself. After about 30 minutes of waiting, we were next up at the gate waiting for the next two cars to come back.

My stomach felt queasy, and my organs felt as if they were playing a game of jacks inside of my stomach. As soon as the ride went up, my organs bounced around, and as soon as the ride came down, some of my organs were left in place, but most of them were inside my throat, so it felt. My husband started to tease me, "You scared, hunh, hunh?" I wanted to punch him in his throat. Approaching second in line, I was sweating bullets. My stomach was doing all sort of things. I felt sorry for whoever was behind me; you could light a match and the whole amusement park would probably blow up since I released so much gas. Finally, as the second car pulled in front of us, I sat down and said a prayer, asking the Lord to please spare my life and my bowels. I sat on the right side (outside) seat, and Ahmad sat on the left inside seat. All there was to secure us was a seatbelt and a lap belt. I put my seatbelt on; I made sure it was nice and tight. Then I pulled my lap belt down, but when I tried to push it up, it wouldn't move. Really freaked out now, I knew there was no turning back.

Not realizing that there was another car in front of us, I felt our car move up and my organs did all types of flips and turns inside of my stomach. I looked at the operator and begged him to please let me off; he looked at me and smiled. All I could do was pray now. I said, "Jesus, Jesus, Jesus."

As you're waiting, there is a traffic light to your right. Just like any other traffic light, you never know when it's going to change colors. It was red; it seemed to be red forever too. As soon as it turned yellow, I tensed my entire body; if you poked me, I probably would have shattered into a billion pieces. As soon as I saw the light turn green, we sped up the hill. I screamed as if I were dying. At one point, I remember my mouth being open, but no sound coming out; it was the craziest thing. Just as soon as I was up the hill, I was back down. I was so wowed at myself for going through with it; all I could do was laugh. It was the most rigorous thing I had ever done. When getting off the ride, my legs were trembling, and I asked my husband, "Can we do that again?" I felt as if I could do any and everything that day.

By Ebony Kelly

Instructor: Dr. Michelle Miller
Took Basic Writing: Spring 2010
Major: Early Child Development
Advice: "Just come to class. Going to the Writing Lab helped a lot, and just write what you feel you know. Let it come natural."

Questions to Inspire Writing

1. Write about your own Cedar Point (or other amusement park) memory.
2. The first time she went to Cedar Point, Ebony was "too chicken" to ride the Top Thrill Dragster. Write about an amusement park ride, sport, hobby, person, etc. that you feel (or felt) too intimidated by to try or approach? Why were you intimidated? Did you conquer your fear? How?
3. Ebony's husband Ahmad encourages and teases her through and past her fear. Write about how someone did something similar for you.

4.   Anticipation is looking forward to something you will enjoy, and apprehension is worrying about what might happen. Ebony anticipates Cedar Point but is apprehensive about Top Thrill Dragster. Write about something you anticipated or write about something about which you felt apprehension.

5.   Ebony faced her fear of riding the Dragster. What fear have you faced and overcome, or did you run away?

6.   After facing her fear of the Dragster, Ebony is so "wowed" by the experience, she wants to ride it again immediately. Did you ever similarly completely change your mind about something?

7.   What scares you? Why? Have you tried (or do you plan) to conquer this fear? How?

8.   What was going through your mind when you read this?

Sibling

I have one sibling, and his name is Michael Aaron Kelly. He is twenty-one years old, and he is a senior at the University of New England in Maine. Michael and I are three years apart, and I think that is just the right amount. In high school and growing up, Michael and I never ever got along. When Michael was a senior and I was a freshman, things really took a turn for the worse.

About halfway through high school, Mike and I would always butt heads. I was never the best student in high school, and he would always call me names such as "retard" and "idiot." Those kinds of things really hurt me, but I would always find some way to cope with it. I was always an average student, but he was continuously the one who got all of the praise. He was a 4.0 student all through high school. That fact would kind of bother me sometimes, but I would try my best and not let it get to me.

When my family and I would go on vacations, I would hope to get closer to my brother. It never happened. I remember asking my mom or my dad why he didn't like me, or why we weren't closer. They would never really have an answer for me. I felt like he didn't have any interest at all in having a brother and sister relationship. Eventually, that thought made me realize that I should just stop trying to make things better. I finally got myself in a mindset where I didn't really care anymore, and if he wasn't willing to try, I didn't want to put in that extra effort because I had already tried with everything I had.

As the years went on, there were ups and downs. There would never be that perfect brother and sister relationship that I had always wished for. I even included it in my prayers at night that maybe one day we could talk and not fight, and my prayers always ended in me asking myself what was wrong with me and why didn't he like me.

When Michael moved away to Maine to attend college, it was very weird for me going from having another sibling in the house to being an only child. I knew he wasn't going to come home much or talk to me, so I was excited at that point because we basically had despised each other for the past four years. Throughout that year, we started to Facebook chat and text. It was a really weird feeling for me, considering our past. We would talk about our parents and things normal brothers and sisters would talk about. I liked it. I would never chat him on Facebook; I would wait for him to chat me. I figured I had tried so much over the past years that I would wait for him to come to me this time. Little did I know, it started to work, and a feeling came over me that I had never had before. It was almost like that brick that had been on my shoulders had finally been taken off. I think the distance helped it a lot.

This past summer of my senior year going into college, Mike came home for the whole summer. At first, it was a bit awkward because we had only talked on Facebook. When graduation for me came around, it started with a picture of us, me in my gown and my brother in his shirt and tie. He told me, "Congratulations" and that he was proud of me; hearing that in person made me teary eyed. It was a miraculous feeling.

Throughout that whole summer, Mike and I began to accept each other a lot more and learned that we had been young, stupid, and ignorant in the past. I was beginning to get to know the brother that I had been missing out on the past four years of my life. It was definitely difficult for me to take in, but I loved every second of it.

Now, my brother is in his senior year of college, and I am a freshman. We talk almost three days a week and like to keep up with each other. We are a lot closer. I think not having a relationship until this past year was really for the best when I put it all into perspective. I think in the long run it made us closer. He is such a successful young man; I look to him for guidance and advice and anything he has to offer to me because it really helps me a lot. I now look at my brother Michael as one of the most important people in my life. I know that I will always think more of him than he thinks of me, but he is such a big role model in my life, so I will love him for who he is now, and not who he used to be. I feel that as the years go on and we both get older and more mature, we will become what I prayed and wished for. Knowing that gives me a great feeling.

By Erin Kelly

Instructor: William Wells
Took Basic Writing: Fall 2010
Major: Business
Advice: "Don't let one bad essay bring you down."

Questions to Inspire Writing

1. Erin writes about her changing relationship with her older brother, Michael. Our relationships with our siblings are often the longest relationships of our lives, and since we grow up with these people, as we change, so does the relationship. Write about the changes you experienced in a relationship with a sibling.

2. When they were kids, Erin's brother called her names. Write about a time when someone called you names and how you dealt with that.

3. For a time, Erin believed her brother didn't like her. Write about a time when you thought someone special to you did not like you.

4. Erin yearned for a perfect sibling relationship. Define and describe such a relationship, and how does yours measure and/or not make the standard? Alternately, what is the perfect parent-child, romantic, or friendship relationship like? Use your own relationship(s) to illustrate.

5. When a sibling or other loved one moves to college, the military, or just away, things change for the family and those in it. How did things change when someone special to you went away? How did things change for others when you went to away (to college or somewhere else)?

6. Erin writes about how she would not initiate a chat with her brother on Facebook but waited for him; she did not want to be rejected. Write about how you carefully limited communication with someone because you worried about upsetting a delicate relationship.

7. It was a special moment when her brother Michael told Erin he was proud of her for graduating high school. Write about a time when someone told you they were proud of you and your reaction to that.

8. Erin's brother Michael is her role model. Who is yours? Why?

9. Erin's relationship with her brother improved after he moved away. We've all heard the expression, "Absence makes the heart grow fonder." Tell a story illustrating this or the opposite truism, "Out of sight, out of mind."

10. What was going through your mind when you read this?

May Forgive but Not Forget

It was a chilly spring morning in April, 2005. I was restlessly lying in bed, unable to sleep. Staring at the ceiling, I was rethinking the past month and a half. I had my hand on my growing belly, knowing that I was not alone in my otherwise empty apartment. At approximately 4:30 am, my cell phone began to ring, and I did not want to answer as I knew what the call would be. I let my voicemail kick in, knowing I would check it as soon as the message indicator went off. Ding, ding, ding, that dreadful tone sounded, and my worst nightmare was about to unfold. It was my very good friend, Robert, whom I had known for years, letting me know that he had found out the truth about my then-husband and his then-girlfriend.

Before getting confirmation from the phone call, my life had already been in shambles. I was basically living alone when I was supposed to be married. The closet that had been full of clothes was a shadow of my husband's coming and goings. Naked hangers where shirts and pants once hung, empty spots where shoes had once been placed, and cleared out drawers were all reminders to me of the brutal past month. I was completely confused by my husband's actions of being vacant from home or only coming home for a few hours and then leaving after a short time. That call was going to explain it all.

I immediately called Robert back, and he briefly explained to me the situation. My now ex-husband, Nick, was having an affair with his now ex-girlfriend, Rachel. Robert had gone over to Rachel's house and found Nick's truck in her garage, hiding, not wanting to be found by Robert and me. For that past month and a half, Nick had been absent from the pregnancy and our marriage. He just up and left with no indication why. He came home once in a while to grab work clothes and other things, but that was it. He told me he wasn't having an affair; however, deep down in my heart I knew he was. I was just in denial.

After Robert was done explaining everything to me, I told him I had to see everything for myself. Robert then came over, picked me up and we headed to Rachel's house. As we were driving, a million thoughts were running a marathon through my mind. My first thought went to what Robert would do to

Nick. Robert was 6'2" and very muscular, not someone you would typically want to be at war with. My

next thought was, Nick and I had been together for eleven years, high school sweethearts. I was eight

months pregnant with our first child, Madelyn, and was also on complete bed rest. We were supposed

to be living that perfect life with that perfect marriage. Anyone standing on the outside looking in was

completely fooled by my incredible acting skills. If someone looked close enough, though, they could see

how miserable I really was, and now I was going to be completely alone.

We got to Rachel's house, where I had decided to confront Nick face to face. Standing on the

road, I could see clearly into Rachel's house. I waited for some sign inside to know that they were up and

awake. Suddenly, the lights came on, and I saw Nick's silhouette moving easily around the house like he

had lived there for years. I knew it was Nick because I could see his tall, lean figure, his dark brown hair,

and one of his nice work shirts from home. There was no way this had been just a casual fling. After

about twenty minutes, Nick walked outside, and the garage door went up. My heart pounded inside of

my chest, and Madelyn started kicking about in my tummy as well. It was unbelievable how she knew

that I was extremely upset. I got out of the car, stepped into the street, and screamed, "Nicholas, how

could you do this?" He stopped dead in his tracks, with one foot in his truck; however, he would not

even turn around. He stood there for what felt like a lifetime and then finally got into his truck, started

it, and began to pull out of the garage. I began yelling again and all the neighbors' lights around Rachel's

house turned on. At that moment in time, I did not even care that I had gotten everyone's attention in

the neighborhood. My life was being destroyed, ripped apart, because two people only cared about

themselves. Robert had to get out of the car and physically drag me back because he was afraid I

wouldn't move as Nick slowly backed down the driveway.

I cried and cried until my tears ran dry. At some point, my tears were so powerful I could not see

through them. I wished Madelyn was already born so I could have someone to love who would love me

back with no questions, no fear. I wanted to experience that unconditional love I always heard about but hadn't known. As Robert and I drove from Cuyahoga Falls to Streetsboro, Nick sent me messages over the phone because he was too much of a coward to call me and speak with me. Even though Nick had been caught, he still tried to lie his way through and say the two of them were "just friends;" however, the truth always comes out. Because of Nick's lies and deceit, we ended up divorcing. I had also found it very hard to trust men in relationships after the ordeal.

It took me about two years, but I did find an incredible man to love and who loves me, and more importantly loves Madelyn also. His name is Chris. Chris has opened up my heart again; I didn't make that very easy for him to do. But Chris was patient, loyal, and trusting while my heart healed. He gave me the time I needed to grieve my ended marriage and my broken heart. And with that time, I began to forgive Nick, but I will never be able to forget.

By Kimberly Lipcsik

Instructor: Mindy Morse
Took Basic Writing: Fall 2010
Major: Respiratory Therapy and Education
Advice: "Don't be afraid to follow your heart with writing."

Questions to Inspire Writing

1. At first, Kimberly was confused by her husband's absence. Write about a time when a loved one's erratic presence—here one time, inexplicably missing another time—confused and hurt you.
2. Kimberly suffers infidelity. Write about a time when someone was unfaithful to you, how you found out, and how things ultimately turned out.
3. "Anyone standing on the outside looking in was completely fooled by my incredible acting skills," Kimberly writes. Write about a time when you had to act one way in public while your feelings deep down inside were very different.

4. With support from her friend Robert, Kimberly confronts her soon-to-be ex-husband and his girlfriend. Write about a time you had to confront somebody.

5. Robert supported Kimberly in her time of trouble. Write about someone who helped you through a tough time.

6. In her pain, Kimberly wishes her unborn daughter was there already so that she could feel that unconditional love. Have you felt that way about parenthood?

7. Kimberly's husband lied and cheated. Has anyone ever hurt you emotionally? Describe. How did you handle the situation?

8. Kimberly finally forgave her husband. Is there someone who wronged you who you were able to forgive? Explain.

9. Kimberly's story starts with a phone call that changed her life. Write about a phone call, letter, email, or text that changed your life.

10. What was going through your mind when you read this?

Who Broke the Typewriter?

"Okay, so who did it? Which one of ya'll broke the typewriter?" My brother O'Neal, sister Myretta and I were all standing there with puzzled looks on our faces like we didn't know what he was talking about. My stepfather, Kenneth Harris, was furious. We paid a visit to his sister Joetta's house in Washington D.C., and while we were there, we had to stay in a back room of her house. The only thing there to play with was a traditional standard typewriter. My sister, brother and I started playing with the typewriter only to find that we had no ink. We looked around and saw a bottle of black Kiwi shoe polish, the scuff kote kind. As kids ages five through seven, we didn't know that shoe polish and a typewriter were a bad combination. We just wanted to type some letters to get through our boring afternoon of being smothered in the back house of Joetta's home. Therefore, we realized instantly that we were in big trouble. We didn't know whether to lie or tell the truth. All we knew is when our stepfather was angry about something, we were in big trouble.

Kenny had a right hand from God; when he would whip you, an instant welt would appear that would sting for days. My mother was afraid to say anything; she would be in the other room clenching her teeth. After time, we had learned how to stuff clothes in our pants and roll around on the floor so that they were hidden; that way the whippings weren't that bad. However, today that wasn't the case. Kenny had caught us off guard, and all we could do was lie.

At first, all we did was stand there. We had faith in each other that no one would tell, but through experience, we've learned that we can't hold out forever; all of us would catch the beating. Sweat and perspiration trickled down our chins. Visible wet spots started to show in our shirts, under our arms, and on our backs. "Well, somebody better say something," he said in a loud thunder roll that made us jump up. My mother just sat there looking at all of us with an expression of helplessness. That let us know that she couldn't do anything about what was about to take place; it was out of her hands.

"What typewriter?" That was the response that came out of my mouth because that was the only response I could think of. I knew full well what they were talking about. The answer popped into my head two seconds earlier. I was just trying to buy time. My mother looked at me with a twisted face in order to say "Yeah, right." Within a flash, I was quickly yoked up by my shirt, my feet were five inches off the ground, and I was face-to-face with the angry Kenneth Harris. His breath smelled of beer and cigarettes; he still had on his work clothes that smelled like oil and engine fuel. His arm was curled up under my chin so far I had no choice but to rest there for a minute, dangle, or choke.

To this day, my assumption is that his sister, Joetta, called him and told him that we broke her typewriter, which caused him to leave work furious. We never expected a day like this to happen, but then again, it was not out of the ordinary. Kenny was mad again. "I done told you about that shit. You know what I'm talking about!" My brother and sister just looked from me to him, flinching to avoid a hit coming their way. I could tell that they were starting to crack under pressure, but I gave them both a look that reminded them that we needed to stick together. It was our only hope. I knew Kenny and how he worked; at an early age, I learned that he wouldn't do anything to us if we all came up with the same story and stuck to our guns. To this day, I still have secret lies that I will surely take to my grave because of the fear of Kenny Harris.

With a thrust, he threw me back down on the floor with a "thud." I quickly got back to my feet and stood back in line. "Myretta," "Kendra," "O'Neal." "Myretta, who did it, tell me something!" He stood there tapping his feet, hands on his hips, with his bottom lip curled up in his mouth snarling towards the heavens, waiting to pounce. He wanted an instant answer, and he wasn't getting it. I closed my eyes, sending a quick prayer to God in hopes that Myretta would stick with the story, or there would be mercy for what was soon to come. Myretta started to stutter. You could hear the desperation in her voice. "Well, well, well, I don't know…"

"That's not the right answer!!!" Within a blink of an eye, Kenny was up in my sister's face. My sister flinched back to cover herself just in case Kenny decided to swing. Spew like a werewolf was flying out of his mouth into her face. At that point, Myretta turned and gave me a helpless look. I didn't know what she was telling me, but the look was like a deer in the headlights. Either she had figured it out that we had to stick to our guns, or she was going to tell in order to get her ass out of hot water. She just bowed her head and replied, "I don't know...." for the last time.

"O'Neal, I know you know what I'm talking about. Tell me something." He took a sip on Blue Bull malt liquor. We could tell that Kenny was starting to break down. Kenny became a lot smoother as his tone lightened, but we knew to still keep our guards up just in case. Kenny's friendlier tactics were known to us. If we confessed now, we knew that we would have broken our secret. O'Neal just shook his head not wanting to say anything; even he knew he couldn't hold water in his mouth. O'Neal has kept very few secrets, so it was best not to tell him anything. After all, he was the youngest.

After one minute and thirty seconds of watching Kenny sip on his beer, there was dead silence in the room. With a deep breath, Kenny told us to go to our rooms until someone told who broke the typewriter. At that point, we really didn't care about staying up in our room; we shot off upstairs and huddled together. We could still hear each others' hearts beat, and we were huffing and puffing from not only being scared to death, but from running up the steps. In a low whisper, O'Neal said his first words "Kendra, you were right. If we stick together, he won't whip us." Myretta shook her head in agreement. Since we all played a part in breaking the typewriter, we all had to stick together.

By Kendra E. Martin

Instructor: Leann Bertoncini
Took Basic Writing: Spring 2010
Major: Civil Engineering
Advice: "My advice to all the writers out there is to tell your story; funny or sad, it's worth telling. Have your own style and detail so that people will never forget it."

Questions to Inspire Writing

1. Children without a toy to play with will make a toy of anything, and in this case, Kendra and her siblings made a toy of an old-fashioned typewriter. Write about a time you played with something that was not a toy and how things turned out.

2. Kendra and her siblings attempted to substitute shoe polish for typewriter ink. Write about a time when you attempted to substitute something for something else with memorable results.

3. Kendra's mother stays in the other room "clenching her teeth" when her husband, the children's stepfather, threatens the kids with a beating if they do not confess. Were the adults in your growing up years in agreement about punishment?

4. Kendra and her siblings attempt denial as a way of deflecting guilt and attempting to avoid punishment. Write about a time when you denied doing something you did. Were you eventually discovered?

5. Write about a time when you were afraid of a parent, step parent, older relative, teacher, boss, or anyone in authority over you.

6. This encounter between the stepfather and the children is a war of wills. Write about a war of wills you were involved in.

7. "Since we all played a part in breaking the typewriter, we all had to stick together," Kendra concludes. Write about a time when something you did with others united you with them in a pact.

8. Describe a time when somebody you thought you could count on let you down.

9. Kendra, Myretta and O'Neal played with the typewriter because they were bored. What are some things you did as child when you were bored?

10. What was going through your mind when you read this?

I Didn't Give up My Goals

The year of 2009, I graduated from Strongsville High School with a 3.6 grade point average. Impressed with my grades at school, my father rewarded my hard work with $1,000 and a ticket to Lebanon for my graduation. I was so excited. The last time I went overseas was when I was six years old. Also, I was thrilled because I've always wanted to have the experience of travelling alone. On June 13, 2009, my mother and grandma took me to the airport. I was happy to leave the country because I needed a break from them, but at the same time I was sad because the next day was my boyfriend's birthday. Naseem, who is twenty years old, is majoring in law, is Lebanese and follows the Muslim religion, just as my family does. My family knows we're dating. He wants to propose to me but not until we are both finished with school.

I stayed in Lebanon at my aunt's house for about two months. My aunt thinks she is the boss of everything. She is very controlling and doesn't accept anyone's opinion; she makes her own decisions. Four different men came and proposed to me while I was there, but I refused them. My aunt invited their families to come without asking my father or me if I wanted to meet them. She told me they were coming after she invited them. Most of them were Lebanese, just like I am. Their families knew mine and found out that Dr. Makki's daughter had come on vacation. One of these men was a 24-year-old dentist, Abbass. He wanted to get engaged to me, but I thought it was really awkward because I was not used to this type of situation, plus I was just 17 years old. His mother called my aunt and told her that their family would like to come to our house because "Abbass thinks Dr. Makki's daughter is beautiful and comes from a respectful family, so he would like to talk to her." The mother said, "If things go well, my son wants to get engaged to her." So Abbass and his family came to my aunt's house. My father was not yet in Lebanon and would not have given his consent for an engagement; therefore, I was stuck between four walls because I could not do anything about the proposal by myself.

Before Abbass's family came, my aunt was telling me to look nice and get dressed up—begging me because she heard from people that he was a good looking man, and many girls liked him. I was very shy and felt hurt because Naseem was waiting for me to return back home. When Abbass and his family came over, I said, "Hi" to everyone and put a fake smile on my face. My aunt was right; he was handsome, but it was strange, and I could not believe what was happening. The others left me alone with Abbass in the dining room while they were drinking tea in the living room. He was talking about what he likes to do and his job. We had some similarities, such as enjoying going to the beach, watching a movie on a rainy day, and shopping. But I could not handle sitting by him and looking into his gorgeous hazel eyes because all I thought about was my boyfriend. I thought to myself, "What am I doing? I can't do this. I love Naseem, and I can't have an engagement ring on my finger when I go back to the United States." I felt like a knife was stabbing me slowly; I felt the deep pain inside me. Abbass told me that he thought I was very cute, nice, respectful, and educated. He told me that he would do everything for me if we got married, such as getting me a house, buying me a car, taking me wherever I wanted to go on our honeymoon, and making me live the most beautiful life ever. It seemed like a dream come true.

I felt like my face was on fire, and I was very nervous. I didn't care about anything that he was saying to me. All I wanted was to have him leave with his family. Finally, he asked me if I wanted to get engaged to him. At that instant, my heart was beating very fast. I felt like I was going to pee in my pants. I said, "Abbass, I understand you and your family are kind people, but I have someone in my life now, and I would like to finish school."

Suddenly, he turned from being happy to being shocked. With a sad, discouraged voice, he told me, "Okay, I hope you live your life, and I don't want to push you. I want you to be excited throughout your life with your love, and I wish the best for you."

I said, "Thank you. Nice meeting you." We both stood up and walked to the living room. We explained to the family that I would like to finish my education, and it is early for me to get engaged.

After that, Abbass and his family thanked us for having them over and left. In my head, I was thinking, "Ugh, finally they left, two hours later."

To me, this was a complicated situation to face because I wasn't used to men coming and proposing to me, but Abbass was only the first one. I could not wait until my father knew about what my aunt did. He would flip out. My family does not want me to get married at this time, and neither do I because I am in school. They want me to have a successful career, and after I accomplish my goals, I can get engaged and married. Also, I refused all the offers of marriage because I am dating Naseem, and I love him so much. Naseem was depressed by this situation. He could not do anything about it because I was so far from him. All he wanted was for me to come back to the U.S. because he thought he was going to lose me.

On July 25, 2009, I arrived back in the States. I was very happy to see everyone, and I missed them a lot. I gave my family their gifts I had gotten them. I saw Naseem, and he told me that he would never let me go back overseas until we get engaged. I agreed because I felt pressured there. I also thought that men were proposing to me because they wanted me to bring them to the United States. These days there are many people wanting to come to America so they can be successful; therefore, I didn't know if they really wanted me to get engaged to them or if they were just using me. It was something to think about. Once I returned, I started school at the University of Akron. I thought to myself that an education is the thing that will lead me to success. First, I should accomplish my goal, then, think about marriage.

By Layale Makki

Instructor: Nora Wagner
Took Basic Writing: Fall 2009
Major: Nursing
Advice: "Basic Writing is a good class. It helps me so much now in my papers. I learned a lot of new techniques with grammar," and her instructor "pushed us to understand and asked us if we had any questions."

Questions to Inspire Writing

1. What has gotten in the way of your holding on to your goals? How have you fought against those people and situations that have tried to make you abandon those goals?

2. In this essay, Layale is away from her family in a distant land in a difficult situation with no one to turn to. Write about a time when you were in a similar situation.

3. Describe your first experience on a plane and/or a time you traveled alone.

4. Have you ever been pressured by a family member (or anyone) to do something you didn't want to do? What were the reasons behind the other person's view as well as your reasons? What were the reasons for the pressure, and how did you feel about it?

5. Do you have a relative or friend who likes to be "the boss of everything"?

6. Write about a significant trip you took.

7. How have family members tried to influence your behavior for good? How have you responded?

8. How have religious and/or cultural differences affected a particular relationship of yours? Describe your differences and how they were or weren't resolved.

9. Layale's experience involves others trying to fix her up when she is already in a committed relationship. Write about fix-ups in your life that either worked or didn't—ones where others tried to fix you up with someone or where you tried to fix up others.

10. Sometimes we find ourselves in what *should* be a dream come true only to realize this is not really *our* dream. Write about your story.

11. Tradition is important to this family and in this story. Do you and your family have traditions you keep and value? Describe and explain.

12. What are the goals you did not give up on? What are the goals you did give up on? Why did you persevere or why did you give up? Tell your story.

13. Write about a long-distance relationship in your life. Were you the person who moved away or the one who stayed? Were you able to maintain the relationship? How? If not, why not?

14. Some of the suitors Layale encounters in Lebanon had ulterior motives, wanting to marry her to come to the United States, for example. Write about a time when you became aware of the ulterior motives of others and how you dealt this.

15. What was going through your mind when you read this?

The Food That Fed My Soul

When I reached the age of six, my grandmother would always cook with me by her side. Everyone knew Mrs. Estella Lacey. Her heart was dedicated to her community, and she would share with anyone who crossed her path. Anyone who was hungry, she fed. I did not know about cooking and prepping all those catering jobs, family dinners, church functions, and even the big clambakes. She gave me the most crucial instructions that have been tools in my life.

In September of 2001, I accepted a job with an independently owned restaurant as a line cook. This changed the path of my career forever. The owner asked curiously if I ever baked any pastries before. She was questioning my ability to bake. The baking instructions I received from my grandmother came in handy. I started to perform this task without using a cookbook. Timidly, I gathered all items and thought," What would be a good cake?" As the entire kitchen staff watched, I mixed a palette-pleasing Neapolitan Cheesecake. The cake baked for 50 minutes and gave the kitchen a delightful fragrance of chocolate and strawberries. I feverishly watched as the owner tasted the cake. "Tammy, this is delicious," she said. The look on her face was angelic, and it made me blush with encouragement. I was offered a new position as Pastry Chef. Modestly, I accepted the job.

The next task was to make soup of the day. I was thinking aloud, "What would be something mouth-watering everyone likes to eat?" When I make soup, chicken and sausage gumbo is my favorite. The recipe is one that turned into a family secret. Smiling, I proceeded with certainty although I had to consider the reactions to a zesty soup. The servers reported that the customers raved about the soup. I received yet another advancement. I excitedly called my mother and asked, "Could you call Grandma and tell her the good news?"

Now I was in charge of making a new soup of the day and daily specials. Every morning I had to make a scrumptious soup. My brain had to recall what the customers liked to eat, the weather, if we had all the ingredients, and I still had to do five lunch specials. I loved what I was doing; therefore, it did not seem to be a stressful task. "I wonder how my grandmother did this for so many years," I asked myself.

Content with my position, I soon became the Kitchen Manager. Wow, I now accepted a lot of responsibility. At five o'clock in the morning, my day started. I dressed myself first and then the children. I had to be the first to arrive to work. This is when the madness began. It started with making the employees' schedules, calling for all food orders and supplies, making sure the kitchen equipment was in good working condition, doing the janitor's job if he didn't, and giving detailed instructions to the employees for the day's prep. Then completing all the specials was still my chore. I thought my life was overflowing with responsibility. It felt like I was a solider marching to war. My grandmother said to me, "Stay true to whatever it is you are trying to do."

My final test arrived, so I thought. The owners accepted a catering job for 2,000 people. Those food-and-people skills my grandmother taught me pushed me through. Frantically doing orders, schedules, hiring extra help, and preparing the food was exhausting. Visualize cooking 2,000 servings of grilled chicken sandwiches, corn on the cob, pasta salad, fresh fruit cups, and cookies. The event was successful and gratifying. I realized at that moment there is nothing that I cannot do.

Holding this position for eight years, I finally had my biggest test of them all. Television news person Robin Swoboda was coming to our restaurant for an interview. I had to cook, prepare, and do the interview. This means I would appear on TV. I was more nervous than I was on my wedding day. I normally do not sweat, but this day I did. When it was time for me to go on camera, my body heated up. I prayed for the words to come out right. As I finished, I gasped for air. Successfully, I had completed another big task. This was not the end; I was on Channel 8 two weeks after the first taped interview. If only my grandmother had seen this job, she would have been proud.

I wish that my grandmother were alive to see my accomplishments today. Grandma would be proud to know that I have never given up. I wonder if in Heaven she can guide my hands. My heart believes so. Now that's food for the soul. I hope you found it scrumptious.

This short story is dedicated to the memory of Mrs. Estella Lacey, a great woman who gave me a survival kit for life.

By Tammy Celeste Millirons

Instructor: Dr. Marjorie Keil
Took Basic Writing: Fall 2010
Major: Hotel Hospitality
Advice: "Write what you feel and don't hold anything back."

Questions to Inspire Writing

1. Tammy learned to cook at the elbow of her beloved grandmother. Write about an older relative who taught you something that you use and value.

2. Tammy enjoys rising to new challenges at her job. Write about how you responded to new challenges at your job. What were the challenges, and how did you respond?

3. Her grandmother said to Tammy, "Stay true to whatever it is you are trying to do." Write about something influential an older relative said to you, and how you applied it in your life.

4. In a high point of her career, Tammy appeared on TV. Have you ever been on television? What were the circumstances?

5. Tammy wishes her grandmother could have seen her at the moment of triumph when she appeared on TV. What moment in your life do you wish that a loved one had been able to witness? Why would that person in particular be able to appreciate that moment?

6. Tammy's life "overflowed with responsibilities." Describe a time (even the present) when your life overflowed with responsibilities.

7. Tammy was very nervous about being interviewed on TV. Describe a time when you were very nervous about something.

8. Tammy's grandmother gave her a "survival kit" of life. Did anyone do this for you? Have you done this for anyone?

9. Tell a special memory of a grandparent.

10. How did you decide on your future career?

11. Who or what influenced your major life decision(s)?

12. Write about a time you were "tested." How did it turn out?

13. Was there a moment when you thought, "There's nothing I cannot do"?

14. What was going through your mind when you read this?

Everything I'm Not Made Me Everything I Am

Recently, I've been looking around, and I notice the spread of Indian culture everywhere. With *Slumdog Millionaire* being such a hit, I see how fascinated the society has become with India. Well, I know when I was a kid, there was nothing I wanted to do but hide the cultural background that made me who I am.

I can say now that I'm more comfortable with who I am as far as being Indian, but it seems that I'm faced with the conflict of being an American as well. I was born in New York, so in a sense, America is all I know. At the same time, I grew up with India all around me. My parents were both born in India and were not hesitant to bring their culture here to the States. My brother Nick and I were indulged with the movies, music and certainly the food. I watch home movies now and notice that at the time, all we spoke at home was Hindi. Being Indian never bothered me when I was young, but I must have reached elementary school when my shame set in.

Our house was filled with my mom's cooking and all the aroma of the spices mixed with my dad's incense in the room where he prayed. I never thought it was weird but was aware that other people weren't the same way. By the age of six, I didn't want Indian food. The glorious sight of a McDonald's Happy Meal with a reward at the end for eating was much more appealing. I loved those toys. My brother was older and knew what to be involved with when it came to American society. I had the privilege to follow what he did.

Around the same time, I was bringing friends home, and there was one girl who I was particularly close to but who never wanted to come over. "Your house smells funny," she said. The words crushed my heart. I immediately became so angry for my parents making us different. We were weird all because of their traditions.

Not long after, I stopped watching Hindi movies and listening to the music. Then I stopped speaking Hindi all together because of an overwhelming shame that was killing my pride. I became so bad about it, that around middle school, I started to tell people I didn't know where my parents were from. When they would ask if I had been to India, it would be a quick yes, and I would shut them off.

I reached high school and knew I couldn't pull off my lies anymore. Nobody ever knew what I meant when I said I was Indian anyway; it was always, "Oh, so you're Native American?" I became so fed up with the confusion that I agreed to whatever people assumed. That same ignorance follows me to this day but still amuses me. My parents were also becoming frustrated with how "American" I was becoming. With my piercings and tattoos, I kept hearing how Indian kids don't do that. Most of the Indian kids we knew were prim and proper and never thought to do such things. I then realized that I wasn't very good at being Indian.

Now with India being plastered everywhere, it's hard to avoid it. I regret the way I acted and wish I could still speak Hindi. All I can do now is understand it when it's being spoken. I do from time to time still get ashamed because of the racism I see. I don't think people realize the intolerance they show when making fun of our accents. Nothing makes me angrier than when people mock the way my parents speak. I wish that people would have a better understanding of the world around them and choose to open their eyes. Hopefully, in the future I can grow in my acceptance and appreciation of who I am and where I come from.

By Jessica Mohan

Instructor: Dr. Michelle Miller
Took Basic Writing: Spring 2009
Major: Fashion Merchandising
Advice: "Be an honest writer and always write what you know. "

Questions to Inspire Writing

1. One's relationship with one's ancestry is important for some people: Write about your ancestry and how it has affected your life.

2. How are you like your parents? Why do you want to be like them? On the other hand, how are you trying to be different? Why do you want to be different?

3. Traditions are important in this household. Have you ever tried to hide your family traditions from friends or others from outside your home? Why? Tell the story.

4. Has any movie or TV show opened your eyes to an important aspect of your own life?

5. Jessica's elementary school friend's critical words about Jessica's family "crush" her heart. Recall the memorable words of someone from your past and the effect they had on you.

6. Write about a memorable time when you and others shared unfamiliar food from another culture.

7. Some cultures have different views of how the younger and older generations should interact. Have you encountered a conflict in how your family and the family of another (a significant other or close friend) view things, and how have you tried to come to a happy medium?

8. Have you disagreed with parents or others regarding tattoos or piercings? Tell your story.

9. What was going through your mind when you read this?

Streetlight Superman

School was out! Most of my friends and I were transitioning from sixth grade to seventh that summer. It was a hot and humid that day, and we were all tired from a rough game of neighborhood football played a couple hours prior. Now bruised and battered, about thirteen of us sat on the front porch and in the front yard of Justin's house. The thirteen of us included David, Cody, Justin, Travis, Alex, a few neighborhood kids and me. We sat there literally lounging around with our feet up and heads back. The streetlights were on, and the sun was about eighty percent set. We sat there, still stinky from earlier, chatting together about school and how we all wanted to meet up at Justin's house for another game of football tomorrow. It was a Friday night, and it seemed at the time none of our parents expected us home for a few hours.

At that point, we all had the same thoughts fluttering through our young minds, "What shall we get into next?" or "What is the plan for the next few hours?" For a moment, there wasn't much talking. Then all at once ideas were shouted out as if we were on Wall Street. "What if we went and toilet papered someone's house?" said Cody.

"Or let's order a pizza and send it to some random address!" Travis said.

"Or we should put Vaseline on a random car window," Alex said. These were ideas we'd all done before.

Only one of many ideas at that time seemed unexplored and caught the majority's attention. I don't know how David came up with this, but he said, "Let's all get in a group, head out to the edge of the road, and when a car comes up the street, we will all pretend to kick the sh*t out of one person. When a car stops, we will all run away." That was the best idea we had heard in a long time.

As we were walking to our place of action, Cody asked, "What are we going to call this game?"

That is when Justin said, "Check it out, the person who gets picked to be the victim doesn't run at first. He has to wait for the person driving the car to get out and ask if he's ok. At that point, he has to stand up, strike a pose with a hand in the air and say, 'I'm okay, I'm STREETLIGHT SUPERMAN!' Then he can run away."

Cody answered back with, "So the game is called Streetlight Superman!" Now, at that point, our excitement level went through the roof!

We got into our positions after Alex volunteered himself for the victim and Superman role that no one else seemed eager to do. Alex then lay down on the side of the street, and we all surrounded him while one person watched for traffic. "Here comes a car!" yelled one of the neighbor kids. KICK, PUNCH, STOMP, KICK, KICK, STOMP!!!!! We were getting our licks in on poor Alex. We didn't just make it look good; we were really beating on him. The only problem was that we didn't get the attention we counted on. The driver was a little old lady, driving a Lincoln, who just slowed down and stared extra hard. We were now all disappointed and stunned.

"Alex, you need to scream for help as they drive by. That time didn't count because there is no old lady I know who would stop her car, get out, and fend off a group of boys twice her size. Let's try it again," David insisted.

Once we gave Alex a chance to stop complaining and recuperate and added a bit more strategy, we were ready for round two. Alex lay back down on the road while we got back into position. "Here comes a truck!" was yelled.

KICK, PUNCH, "SOMEONE HELP!" KICK, KICK, PUNCH, STOMP!!!!! Sure enough, this time, about four feet from us, the dark-colored truck came to a screeching halt! Those skidding tires were all we needed to hear. We then ran as fast as we could, just far enough away to still see and hear the courteous citizen ask Alex if he was okay. Then we watched her jump back in surprise after the once hurt little boy sprang up, struck a Superman pose, yelled something about the streetlights, and then ran away. We then as a group, waited for Alex to catch up, only to run away in pure laughter as the confused woman got back in her truck to drive away.

By the next summer, with plenty of practice and no police trouble, we had outgrown the Streetlight Superman game, but it still makes for a good story. From time to time, I think about driving down the road and coming across this same type of tomfoolery, and what I would do as an adult in that strange situation. My guess is I'd probably laugh with them. I don't think I'll ever grow up. It was just too much fun.

By Aaron Mulligan

Instructor: Dr. Michelle Miller
Took Basic Writing: Summer 2010
Major: Construction Engineering Technology
Advice: "Have fun turning your words into a movie."

Questions to Inspire Writing

1. Aaron writes about that magical moment that middle school students treasure: the beginning of summer vacation. Write about a special beginning-of-summer vacation memory of your own.

2. Write about a time when you and a group of friends, a bunch of bored kids, came up with a brilliant idea for relieving your boredom.

3. Aaron and his friends put on a demonstration for strangers to make a scene and see what happens. Write about a time when you (alone or with others) put on a similar scene and what kind of reaction you got.

4. Aaron and his friends enjoyed the Streetlight Superman game for one summer before they outgrew it. Write about a similar activity or game you enjoyed for a period in your life before you outgrew it.

5. Aaron wonders what he would do if he encountered another group of kids playing a prank like the one that he and his buddies played. Did you ever encounter something like this? Was it a prank? How did you know? Did you become involved? How did you react?

6. Kids, especially at the middle school age, enjoy playing with adult reality and trying things out, being experimental. Write about similar experiments of your own.

7. What childhood games did you play out in the neighborhood?

8. Did you or anyone you played with get hurt while playing a childhood game? Write about that.

9. What was going through your mind when you read this?

Achieving My G.E.D.

I was just your average student attending Garfield High School. I was not a popular person in school, but I did have a lot of friends. In high school, I had three very close friends, Tati, Simi, and Janeen. We all met in the 9th grade; we were all bad influences on each other from the day we met. We used to flick (miss) school often without our parents knowing. We all would catch the bus to Rolling Acres Mall to hang out. Rolling Acres was a hot spot for young kids to hang out. Also, our chances of seeing someone we knew were very slim. As young, unruly kids, we did not have a clue that missing so much school would reflect in our grades. By 9th grade midterm, my grades suffered badly from missing so much school. I soon realized that hanging out at the mall so much was not the thing to be doing. I personally came to the conclusion that I needed to give my bad-influence friends a break. I had to separate myself from them. I needed and wanted to focus on my education. Luckily, I was able to pull my grades up to average level and pass to the 10th grade.

At the beginning of my 10th grade year, my mother's health began failing and she became unable to walk. By the end of my 10th grade year, my mother had to have major surgery. As a result of my mother's health failing, I felt obligated to take care of my mom. I have an older sister, Crystal, who at the time had her own family to care for. She was a single mother working full-time at Rubbermaid. She barely maintained her own household. Crystal was unable to care for my mother daily. My father, Eddie, was the only person bringing in income to maintain our household while my mother was sick. My father owns a mechanical car repair shop that's open daily 8am- 6pm. My father was unable to care for my mother during the day. Anyone else outside of our immediate family was not acceptable for helping my mother because of mother's own personal privacy issues.

I was raised with the concept being instilled in me as a young kid that "Family Is First." So I was willing to sacrifice my education to take care of my mother. As an educator, my mother was not happy at all with my willingness to drop out of school; however, it was necessary. In all, it ended up taking about three months for me to nurse my mom back well. Once my mom was back on her feet, I attempted to go back to school, but I was way behind. My confidence for being able to complete to 10th grade was shot. I knew I would be made fun of if I repeated the 10th grade, so I never returned.

After officially dropping out of school and being 18 years old, I never felt the pressure of needing to get a G.E.D. I was faithfully able to keep a fast food job. I worked at Taco Bell, Burger King, etc., but I was growing tired of working at fast food places. I soon came to realize their hiring requirements/standards weren't too high, so I wanted the feeling of importance that comes with a real job. Even with no high school diploma and only fast food experience, I still continued to look for work. By the great goodness of God, I found a great job at Giant Eagle Pharmacy, where I started out as a bagger. After one year I became a Pharmacy Tech, which came with on-the-job training. I was employed with Giant Eagle for six years. I was always on time, dedicated to my job, and just an all-out perfect example of a great employee. In 2009, Emily's Law went into effect and required that every tech in the State of Ohio be certified by the State Board of Pharmacy. When it became time to be certified, I didn't qualify because I didn't have a G.E.D. or Diploma. I lost my job for not being qualified to hold the position. It was a sad day in the Giant Eagle Pharmacy when I lost my job. The mood in the pharmacy that day was disturbed and emotional. My manager, Greg, was in tears; he always referred to his employees as his children. Greg was older in age and experience; he was our peacemaker and father figure. A few of my co- workers shed tears with me. I kept in touch with mostly everyone from work through Facebook.

Getting my G.E.D. became my new goal. My search had begun to find a great G.E.D. program. I heard a lot of good things about a program called Project Learn. I went and signed up for classes, Monday-Friday 5 p.m.-8 p.m. daily. I attended classes at Project Learn for three months before getting my G.E.D. Project Learn has a very pleasant learning environment. I do believe my teacher Ms. Bobbie's support, one-on-one help, and encouraging words played a big part in my success. I studied long and hard to be able to understand the material needed to pass the G.E.D.

I took my G.E.D. test January 6, 2010; I passed it. I chose to take my test in Canton, Ohio. I was informed that the Canton test-taking areas are usually not as full. On the day I took my G.E.D. test, we had a terrible ice storm that came across the area. I can remember driving at 20 mph in my car on the expressway to take my G.E.D. test in Canton, Ohio. The actual G.E.D. test was 8 hours in length, split up in two days, four hours each day. I had to make two trips to Canton in that ice storm. There were so many students who called, postponing their test because of the weather. I was determined to get to the testing center. There were a total of eight people in the same class that showed up for the test. I over-prepared by over-studying; I did not know what to expect. The test was not as hard as I studied for. I passed the G.E.D. test with all high scores.

My motivation and support came from my family. My family is very proud of me since I had achieved my G.E.D. As a school teacher, my mother felt it was important that I get my G.E.D. At the time, my sister, Crystal, and my mother both supported me financially because of my job loss. My sister and mother provided me with the gas money to be able to get back and forth to the G.E.D. classes. Crystal paid for me to be able to take the G.E.D. test, and she was just like my personal tutor. If I needed help with anything, I knew I could count on my mom and sister. I wanted to make sure I succeeded at getting my GED for myself and family for all their hard work and for believing in me.

I felt the need to get my G.E.D. for a sense of achievement, to find a good job, and to attend college. I didn't want to go on in life feeling incomplete like I was only worth a McDonald's job because I didn't have my G.E.D. Getting my G.E.D. set the stage for me to obtain my next goal, which was to attend college. Here I am today, proud to say I'm a college student at The University of Akron. I have met a lot of nice people here at college, and I'm also making wiser choices about the friends I make. I will remain focused throughout school, just as I did when I obtained my G.E.D. I'm taking beginners' classes in the basics like Basic Writing and College Reading and Study Skills. Next year, I will take courses that will lead me to being an Independent Licensed Social Worker. Failure is not an option.

By Rebecca Patten

Instructor: Dr. Michelle Miller
Took Basic Writing: Fall 2010
Major: Social work
Advice: "Stay focused. Don't be afraid to use the Writing Lab. That was the biggest thing that helped me."

Questions to Inspire Writing

1. Achieving her G.E.D. is a precious academic prize for Rebecca. Write about an academic achievement of yours.

2. In Rebecca's teen years, the family responsibility of taking care of her mother came first. Write about a time when school was put on a back burner to needs more pressing at the time.

3. What obstacles got between you and your education?

4. Another of Rebecca's obstacles came from friends who were bad influences. Write about bad influences from your past.

5. What were your school attendance habits like? Why were they like that? What was the outcome?

6. Rebecca was raised with the idea that "Family is first." What ideas were you raised with, and how did those ideas play out in your day-to-day life?

7. Going back to high school was not easy for Rebecca. Did you ever leave school for awhile and attempt to return? How did it work for you?

8. Despite having no high school diploma, Rebecca was able to find a job she liked at a pharmacy, but then she was disqualified for this job because of a new law. Did you ever lose a job due to similar circumstances? Write about that.

9. What are the kind of jobs you can get with your current level of education, and what kinds of jobs could you get with a little more education, and what kind of jobs could you get with a lot more education? How much education do you think you should get to fulfill your professional goals?

10. Studying for her G.E.D. with Project Learn was one of the most successful parts of Rebecca's educational experience. Write about the most successful part of your educational experience.

11. Rebecca writes that her family provides her motivation and support. What is your source of motivation and support?

12. Have you ever "taken care of" a family member or other person close to you?

13. Have you ever made a sacrifice for the benefit of someone else? Or has someone done that for you?

14. Write about getting or losing a job.

15. Write about a memorable boss, supervisor, mentor, "father figure," or "mother figure."

16. What are your long-term goals? What short-term goals will help you reach the long-term goals?

17. When in your life was "failure not an option?" What did you do to ensure success?

18. What was going through your mind when you read this?

"You Can't Have Your Cake and Eat It Too."

My Aunt Georgia always said, "You can't have your cake and eat it too." Until recently, I never quite understood the expression. I always thought that if the cake was yours, you can have it and eat it whenever you please. Of course, eventually it will be gone or go bad, but you did have it and were able to eat it whenever you wanted to. Georgia would say this to me when I was a little girl, and I would always argue with her that it could be done. I never realized there is such a bigger meaning behind the metaphor.

As an adult, I totally understand the meaning now. Someone can work their whole life for a beautiful home, and they will never get to enjoy it because they have to work so hard just to be able to afford it. I think a lot of people have learned the meaning of this metaphor by thinking the way that I did as a child. Everyone wants the finest things in life; however, they cannot appreciate them when they have worked so hard just to get those things. I believe it is human nature to always want more than what you have. When I first moved into my new house, I wanted everything new. I wanted the biggest TV with the best entertainment center and the best furniture. I knew that in order to have all those things, I would have to slowly accumulate them. I moved all my old furniture into my new home and just had the basics. I started out with the old TV I had from my parents and a set of used $300 furniture that looked nice but certainly wasn't up to my standards. After being settled in for a few months, I decided to make a list of everything I needed. On the back of my list, I wrote all the things I wanted to replace. Of course, my list of wants was a lot longer and more expensive than my short list of needs. I started saving my extra money in a jar above the refrigerator. I was in a hurry to have nicer things, so I saved every extra dime I had.

A big flat screen TV was the first thing I bought. I wanted it so bad that when I had enough money, I set out to get one that day. Instead of doing the smart thing like watch the ads and price out every one I saw, I went straight to the stores. I went to two stores before I purchased it. I was so set on buying my new TV that I forgot I needed a truck to get it home. I was at Best Buy all checked out with my 42" flat screen. I walked it outside and realized it wasn't fitting in my small car. I thought to myself, "Good job, Katelin! Now you have your TV. How are you going get it home?" I called my dad to come pick up the TV for me and bring it to my house. He was upset that I bought it because he thought there were more important things I could have spent the money on. He told me that I should have bought new pots and pans and a new stove instead. I didn't care about those things because what I had I thought was good enough. The following week, Wal-Mart had a bigger TV on sale for less than what I paid for mine. I never checked the prices until after I had the one I bought, which goes to show, I was too worried about buying one that I didn't care what I spent. I didn't think about what else I could have had instead. I wanted that piece of cake, and I wanted it now.

I was back at square one, starting my savings all over again. This time I was set on new furniture for my living room. My walls are blue, and my carpet is gray. I had a set of dark green furniture that I just couldn't wait to put on the curb. I told my aunt Georgia to keep a look out on some nice furniture I could buy to make my living room look good. She said, "You need to save up a $1,000 and put it in your savings first. Then after you have that saved you can start saving for new furniture."

I asked "Why?"

She replied, "Every homeowner should have at least a $1,000 set aside just in case something in your house needs repaired or fixed." I thought by the time that I had that much money saved, it would be over six months before I could get new furniture. I decided against her advice. I thought everything in my house was fine, and nothing would break. I figured I would save the extra $1,000 after I had new furniture.

The day came when I went and bought my new furniture. I knew I had to have it the moment I saw it. It is dark brown, overstuffed, reclining matching sofas. I knew it would go perfect because my living room is so big. I spent way more that I intended to. I just couldn't help it. They cost me $1,400. This time I had them delivered. That way I wouldn't have to hear my dad's crap about me blowing my money on it. The furniture came, and I had it for about a month. I decided I already had the things I just had to have, so I wasn't putting any money aside. I was living paycheck to paycheck, paying my bills, buying food, spending the rest on clothes, and other little things I felt like buying.

One day I was standing at the sink doing dishes, and I realized my hot water wasn't working. I went to the basement and saw the pilot light was off. I called my dad. He came over that day to look at it. He got it lit, but the next day, it was back to no hot water. My dad, who knew he didn't know much else about it, had my Uncle Joe come look at it. Joe works for a heating and cooling company. The hot water tank was broken. Joe said it was going to be cheaper and easier to buy a new one because mine was working on nine years old. We went to Home Depot, and the cheapest 40 gallon gas water heater was $900. I only had a little over $300 in my bank account. In order to get the rest, I was going to have to borrow the money. Of course, Georgia is the one to go to when you need to borrow money. Oh, man, did I hear it from her when I told her I never saved the $1,000 she told me to. She yelled, "Now, Katelin, didn't I tell you to save that money before you went out and bought new sofas?"

I said, "Yes, Aunt Georgia, I'm a moron. The last thing I was thinking about was my hot water tank." I basically had to say, "You were right, and I was wrong." After my getting yelled at for a while, she agreed to loan me the money. We agreed that I would pay her $100 a week for six weeks.

What I've learned from my experience is, when you buy things on impulse, you're likely to regret your decision down the road. Now, when I have the urge to spend my money that I worked hard to save, I sit down and ask myself, do I really want that? Is it worth the money? Is it necessary? Is there anything I really need instead? By asking myself those questions, I usually end up talking myself out of buying the thing I think I want. The moral of my story is don't be in a hurry to buy things that can wait. Always have money saved in case something goes wrong. Listen to your elders because they are always right. Don't work too hard for things you want. Enjoy what you have. Remember, "You can't have your cake, and eat it too!"

By Katelin Puzakulics

Instructor: Dr. Michelle Miller
Took Basic Writing: Fall 2010

Questions to Inspire Writing

1. "You can't have your cake, and eat it too" Is a famous old saying. Find an old saying that brings up a memory for you and tell your story.

2. Katelin describes her goals when she moved into her first house. Describe what you wanted for a new residence of yours, whether it is a house, an apartment, a room in a residence hall, or even a room at your childhood home that was your own after a sibling-roommate moved out.

3. Katelin saved her money for a big screen TV; have you ever saved money for a particular goal? What was the goal, did you make it, and if so, when and how did you get it?

4. Hoping to take her new TV home on her own, Katelin found out she could not fit it in her car and had to swallow her pride to ask her father, who is critical of her purchase. Write about a time when you did something impulsively, hadn't thought things through, and had to ask for help from someone who gave you a difficult time.

5. After she achieves a financial goal of buying new furniture, Katelin has an emergency of a broken water heater. Write about an unexpected financial emergency you had to face and how you dealt with it.

6. Write about a time you had to borrow money.

7. Katelin says she believes "it is human nature to always want more than what you have." Write about an experience of yours that would demonstrate/show that you agree or disagree with Katelin.

8. Like Katelin's experience of buying her big screen TV, have you ever made an impulsive purchase or made an impulsive choice, rushing into something and possibly regretting it later?

9. As you were growing up, what did you learn and/or observe about money, saving, spending, buying habits, priorities, etc.? How did these practices, values, and attitudes influence you? Did you "follow in those footsteps?" Did you take the opposite route?

10. Were you ever in a "big hurry" to grow up, to reach a goal, or to get somewhere?

11. Katelin writes, "The moral of my story is, don't be in a hurry to buy things that can wait. Always have money saved in case something goes wrong." Is this advice you follow?

12. Katelin had a big list of "wants" for her new home. What's on your list of "wants"? What are you doing to get them?

13. Katelin regrets buying things for her home on impulse. Have you ever regretted doing anything on impulse? Explain.

14. What was going through your mind when you read this?

My First Day of Kindergarten

"Girls, wake up. It's 7:00!" Mark exclaimed.

My husband always wakes up so happy in the morning. I crawled out of bed; today was September first, my first day of kindergarten. Realizing Summer was already in her room getting dressed, I finished getting ready. She was dressed in less than seven minutes.

"What's next?"asked Summer.

"Medicine," Mark said.

Summer had a bug a week before, but she was feeling a lot better.

"Do you need help with anything else before I leave?"asked Mark.

"Nope, I can brush her hair and teeth," I said. "Enjoy work today."

He was out the door, and I had to finish getting Summer ready.

"Let's go brush our teeth and your hair, Summer," I said.

"Okay, Mommy," Summer said.

After we brushed our teeth and her long brown curly hair, we went out into the kitchen.

"Do you want anything for breakfast?" I asked. I already knew the answer, but I had to ask. Summer doesn't like breakfast food so early in the morning.

"No, Mom," she stated so calmly.

She wasn't nervous about the first day of kindergarten, so I wasn't going to be either. We've done this before; I've dropped her off at the babysitters' and preschool. Today was different; no one would be there to help her or protect her. My heart was starting to hurt, but I knew she was ready for the first day of kindergarten. I got her Scooby Doo lunch box down, and she started to pack her own lunch. She was a big girl, and she was acting like one too.

Summer and I gathered up all of our bags. We made our way outside to the Cobalt. She was carrying her Little Pet Shop book bag and her Scooby Doo lunch box. She looked like a little girl with her corduroy skirt, white short-sleeved blouse, white ankle socks, and her no-tie Skechers. Her curly hair was in a ponytail, and she had a smile from ear to ear.

"Are you ready for kindergarten, Summer?" I asked.

"Yes, Mom. When are Sean, C.J. and Jules going to be there?" she happily shouted.

I explained, "Grandma, Aunt Amy, Aunt Amber, Uncle Steve, and your cousins will all be there."

The excitement in the car grew greater as we made our way to school. Then we parked across the street from Betty Jane Learning Center in a plaza parking lot along with other parents. Our family started to pull in; everyone started to unpile from their cars and gathered in the middle of the parking lot. Sean, C.J., and Jules, her cousins, all looked nice in their new school uniforms. There was excitement in the air. It was the first day of school. We started to walk across the street, and each child grabbed an adult's hand. I made sure I grabbed Summer's because our minutes together were running short.

I asked again, "Are you ready for the first day of kindergarten?"

"Mom, I'm ready," she exclaimed.

We started to walk behind the school to stand in line for room 112, Mrs. Toth. Parents were standing there with their children to start their first day of school. Today was other parents' first day of kindergarten also. Line by line, each class started to go inside Betty Jane. C.J. was in her class, so Amber and Steve walked in front of us. Summer and I walked to Room 112.

Summer walked into her classroom that had little tables and chairs. Kindergartners had their own little bathroom, a rug to read stories, and a play area. She grabbed a dog bone that had her name with a piece of yarn attached and put it on over her head. She didn't ask me for help. I signed a piece of paper stating she was a car rider not a walker or day-care child.

"Put your lunch boxes in the blue container, and put your book bag in your locker with your name," Mrs. Toth explained to her new kindergartners. "Then go sit at a table."

Summer did exactly what she was told. She put her lunch box in the blue container and her book bag in her locker.

Afterwards, she went and sat down at the green table with C.J. , who was sitting across from her. Then these little strangers whom I didn't know sat around her. She started to play with Play Doh and a little man cookie cutter that was on the table in front of her. She was ready for me to leave. My family was already gone, and I wanted to make it to my second college class.

"I love you! Have a good first day of kindergarten. I will pick you up after school is done," I said.

"I love you, too, Mommy!" she happily said. "See you after school."

I walked to the door, just stood there, standing there waving goodbye which wasn't long enough, but I knew I had to leave. It was my first day of kindergarten.

By Ashley Saulic

Instructor: Andrea Scott
Took Basic Writing: Fall 2010
Major: General Business
Advice: "I would say listen to your professors and don't be scared about writing."

Questions to Inspire Writing

1. The conclusion of Ashley's essay makes clear that the first day of school belongs to parents as well as the children. If you are a parent, write about how you experienced a first day of school with your child or children, and if you are a student, write about a memorable first day of school in your life.

2. Summer, Ashley's daughter, is excited in part at the prospect of the friends she has whom she knows she will see at school. Write about the role school friends played for you. Did they make school more fun for you, did they distract you, or both? Write about your experience with friends at school.

3. Describe a memorable first day of school—kindergarten, middle school, high school, or college.

4. Ashley recalls her daughter's first day of kindergarten and the pain of "letting go" of her little girl. Can you recall a time you had to let someone you loved go on without you?

5. Several members of Ashley and her daughter Summer's extended family come to meet the mother and daughter in the parking lot across from school to support the little girl on her first day of kindergarten. Write about the ways your family (or did not) support you at an important time in your life.

6. Summer went to school with cousins. Write about memories of yours where family (siblings, cousins, parents, etc.) combined with school.

7. Ashley feels a slight twinge as she sees her daughter independently do things without her help. If you are a parent, write about a similar moment of your own. Or, writing from the child's point of view, write about a time when you acted independently from your parents and how they reacted.

8. What was going through your mind when you read this?

A Long Drive Home

One extremely boring night with a head full of unwanted thoughts, I found myself unable to steady my mind enough to fall asleep. I decided the only way I could rid myself of those night-time day-dreams was to go for a long drive somewhere I have never been before. It made sense at the time that if I was lost in my head, I might as well be lost in real life. I grabbed two energy drinks, a Cliff Bar, and an mp3 player filled with thousands of songs that best fit my mood to begin on my mind-freeing journey.

Starting off small, I drove to a part of Akron I had never been before; some might call it a "shady area." I drove around for about ten minutes; I thought I heard gun shots and a faint hellish scream coming from a distance. It was about that time I realized that trying to get lost in a bad part of Akron at 2:00 a.m. might be a bad idea; I quickly hopped on the highway and headed north. Driving on Route 8 was pretty soothing at such a late time of night. There were no blinding bright lights coming from passing cars or road-raged citizens following too close behind me because I accidently drove the speed limit when I should have been driving faster. There was nothing besides The Shins whispering to me every once in awhile through my tiny speakers when the gushing wind coming in the window decided the time was right to let the hypnotic melody play through. I was king of my own domain in those small stolen minutes of time; nothing could stop me, nothing at all. Then without any preemptive warning, burning blue and red lights demanded my attention. I sat there praying to the road gods at the top of my mind's lungs, "Please! Please! I do not knoweth what I did to offend thee! Please! Please! Let this terrible man go away!"

A striking fear rushed over me; nothing but the silence of beading sweat only audible in my mind rolling down my forehead and the vague "tick-tick" of my car's hazard lights were heard. My mind quickly flashed back to the numerous times I was pulled over by the cops for suspicion, without any valuable evidence, of being intoxicated or under the influence of some sort of drug. I realized later that those situations were frequently at the end of the month, where some of us regular citizens assume the police are low on tickets and need to meet a quota. Whether or not this is entirely true, I do not know. Since this instance happened to fall on the 28th, I found myself not too surprised that I was being pulled over; nonetheless, it didn't prevent me from being any more scared than I already was.

Blinded by the evil man's white light of doom, I was aware he was standing right beside my car, looking down through my side window judging me and sure enough searching for something to "make his day." Gauging by his slight chuckle, the creeping speed of my manual window made me look pathetic in the eyes of this great man of the law. Soon as my window had finally done its job of taking away all that was left of my self-dignity, the man barked, "What are you doing?" From this question, I only could assume he was interested in the whole story of what brought me to that exact point in time.

"Well, you see... I couldn't sleep, so...."

He abruptly interrupted without allowing me time to explain myself. "You couldn't sleep so you decided to drive around getting into no good and doing drugs. Is that what I'm hearing from you, boy?" the officer shouted.

Stunned and very confused, I replied with, "Uh....what?"

"I know what you kids like to do nowadays. There is no fooling me! There's a reason why dey made me da Sherriff!" Still dumbstruck, I could only get out a short "......" before he laid back into me, "You kids have no respect for da law or elders for dat matter! Ya'll think you can do whatev'r feels good. Snortin' rock, suckin' blow, yeah... I bet you didn't count on me knowing what all dose thangs were, did ya!?"

Finally coming back to consciousness, I was able to muster up an actual sentence: the only logical explanation for these unreal words coming from a man that is paid by the government to protect and serve us, the citizens of the United States, was that he must have been drunk. Using that as logic, I asked the question, "Are you drunk, sir?"

He looked at me with the same look a dog gives his master when the beast is asked a question. After a few minutes of staring at one another, he retorted with seven little words: "Don't let me be catchin' you again."

He turned around towards his noise-maker mobile 3000, and after attempts to get in, his left foot catching itself briefly between the closing door and the car, he drove off. I sat there for a few moments, stupefied. For awhile, I thought I might have dreamt it out of sheer boredom, or that it was a hallucination brought on by all of the Red-Bulls I had consumed. While attempting to collect the pieces of my mind that were scattered all over the front end of my car and trying to think of some sort of logical explanation for what had just taken place, I took a long deep breath, punched in the double red triangle that made the tick ticking noise that was softly reverberating through my empty car, and headed on my way up the lonely road once more.

Clearing my head of the nonsensical foolery that just took place, I headed farther north until I felt I had run up the highway long enough. I pulled off at an exit labeled Bishop Avenue, thinking that a cop would never follow me down a road named after a person who is a man of the cloth. I took an immediate right followed by a left, then another left. I drove halfway down

160

that last stretch of road until I saw a beautiful white face slightly peering through a ray of

moonlight, hidden by a few tree branches, and just above a row of ill-kept shrubbery. I carefully

pushed on the brake pedal in hopes that the loud echoes, a result of being in a cluster of houses

in the sparse summer's night air, of my diesel engine and screeching worn-out brake pads

wouldn't awaken the sleeping dogs down the vast stretch of houses. I flipped my stick into

reverse, backed up a few yards, then flipped it back to first. When I turned my headlights on the

brightest setting, I discovered an unlit driveway leading up to an empty parking lot. Curiosity

killed the cat, but since I was no cat, I decided it would be quite all right to do some exploring. I

rolled down both of my windows to bring in the fresh air as I drove down the long, narrow, and

unfamiliar driveway; I smelled freshly cut grass and newly laid mulch. I finally reached the end

of the road, which was tinier and half the size of other roads, and entered into the parking lot.

From what I could see, I assumed I was at some sort of church or a Catholic high school

perhaps. I found a parking spot right in front of the white statue, which ended up being Mother

Mary, and put my car in park. I sat there for quite some time thinking about everything that was

plaguing my mind, what had just happened to me, where I was at that moment, and finally

where I was in life. I prayed for the first time in years that night, not counting the time I was

praying to the road gods; I asked for guidance, strength, and the possibility of receiving a

blatant sign of what I should do next. I prayed so long and so hard that I didn't even realize I

fell asleep with my keys still in the ignition.

I woke up with a symphony of chirping, which came from the tremendous amount of

birds that were perched on the branch hanging above my car. Judging by the attitude my car

had from my constant turning of the ignition, I quickly realized my car was unresponsive and

most likely dead to the world. Figuring my battery had failed me, I set off to look for someone to help me bring this metal beast back from Death's door by sending a jolt of electricity through its Frankenstein body. I walked around to the front of the building and knocked on a set of glass doors with strange inscriptions all over them. A man in black came to the door, greeting me. "Hello, I'm Father Bob. What can I help you with today?"

I told him about my car and how my battery seemed to be dead. He jumped into action, immediately knowing what to do. "Hold on just a second," he said with a large smile. "I'll be right back."

Father Bob returned with a set of jumper cables clenched between his right elbow and his rib cage. We walked out to the parking lot together, talking while we ventured out to my motionless car. He told me all about the building I spent the night parked in front of, informing me that it wasn't a high school but a seminary for Catholic priests. Comforted by his kindness, I decided I could confide in him about all of my inner turmoil, about how I always had a thought in the back of my mind about the priesthood, and about how that thought had been buried deep within my consciousness as result of the poor choices I had already made in my life. I just assumed someone with my past experiences would be frowned upon by others if I would decide to consider the seminary. He then looked at me, pointed at the ground and said with sincerity, "This parking lot has just been recently repaved, covered in layers of black tar and rock. Through all of that, a flower still manages to emerge from a crack in the pavement, overlooked by those who laid the tar." My eyes found the beautiful flower that my mind refused to see before; after viewing that flower, I would never forget the shy blue petals peeking through the rocky bed.

He told me that great men of religious faith have always been found in unexpected places. Some came from sheltered lives with no previous knowledge of being homeless or alone; a few came from darker places where there were no signs of light at the end of the tunnel. Those men had the courage and the strength of God to keep looking for what they were missing in their lives and to help those who might have lost their way.

He posed a question to me, asking if I really thought what a man did before he became a priest actually mattered. Without a clue on how to answer this, I gave him a slight shrug of the shoulders. Predicting I would reply in such a manner, he trucked along, telling me that he believed those poor decisions and bad experiences would make the priest great, making the priest human and allowing that man to relate to others who are in similar situations. The next thing that fell from his lips sent tiny needles down my spine, a sentence that I will not soon forget, "The only way to find out if you are that type of man who is called to greatness is to embrace your past and all of your fears, to take a chance with the unknown. You need to ask yourself, are you that flower that survived through the crack in the rocks?"

There wasn't much conversation after he asked that final question. Our attentions were focused on the task at hand, the incapacitated car. Normally, when I am faced with silence with a stranger, I become uneasy and anxious; this instance was different. I felt at peace and meditative.

After we successfully jumped my car, we said our brief goodbyes, and I expressed my great appreciation for his help. Before I was able to roll up my window all the way, he stole my attention once more, offering an invitation to a dinner with himself, a few others, and the bishop of the Cleveland diocese the following Sunday night. I graciously accepted and thanked him for his invitation. From that point on, for about two years, I would end up at that parking lot every Sunday; I would meet up with students, talk to faculty, or just simply sit in solitude in a partially empty parking lot with a beautiful white face that once peered through a ray of moon-

light just so it could change my life forever.

By Jonathan Wade Wilcox

Instructor: Nora Wagner
Took Basic Writing: Fall 2010
Major: Information Technology
Advice: One, "Don't let anyone tell you how to write; only let them teach you how to write properly." Two, "Write what you know. If that fails you, then write what you want to know." Three, "Everyone has an opinion. Don't take them too seriously."

Questions to Inspire Writing

1.   Write about a memorable long drive you once took.

2.   How do you clear your head?

3.   Have you ever gotten lost?

4.   The flower that survived through the crack in the rocks is a metaphor for Wade's survival. Do you have a story of survival—your own or that of someone or something close to you?

5.   Write about an experience with seeing a "sign," feeling a "calling," or something that seemed supernatural or spiritual.

6.   Have you ever experienced the kindness of a stranger(s)?

7.   On his drive, Wade is stopped by a police officer who appears to want a driver to "make his day" and accuses Wade of doing drugs. When Wade politely asks the officer if he had been drinking, the officer retreats. Write about a memorable time when you were stopped by the police.

8.   Wade turns the tables on the officer; write about a time when you reversed the advantage with an authority figure.

9.   Wade took a ride to help him relax. What do you to relax or help yourself fall asleep?

10.   Wade's prayer to the Mother Mary statue seems to have come true. Has God ever answered your prayers?

11. Wade quotes Father Bob and says those words were unforgettable to him. Have anyone's words to you been as memorable, powerful or influential?

12. This essay illustrates a life-changing event. Can you recount a life-changing moment from your own life?

13. What was going through your mind when you read this?

Man, I Love Cowboy Boots!

Imagination is one of those things that children have over adults. When you were little, did you ever dream of being the world's next super-hero like Spiderman or Superman but faster, stronger, and overall more super? Maybe you were more of a level-headed kid and dreamed of being a doctor, policeman, fireman, or lawyer, which are all great professions. As a kid, I never dreamed of being super or having a wonderful profession. As far back as I can remember, all I ever dreamed of was being a cowboy.

Obviously, it all started with my dad, Frank W. Yancey, watching cowboy movies on Saturday morning with me. I could see myself riding a horse across the open planes of the Wild West. Without a doubt, the one I remember the most is *Lonesome Dove*. Strangely, it was an eight-hour movie, and at five years old, I could sit down and watch the whole thing. When I would watch the movie, it was as if I was inside the TV, living the life of a cowboy. I imagined sleeping under the stars and cooking biscuits over a campfire. I loved the idea of being a cowboy so much that I needed something they had. I knew that a horse was out of the question, but what about some cowboy boots? My little five-year-old mind began to wonder. Then I could be a cowboy just like my heroes on *Lonesome Dove*.

Growing up, my family did not have a money tree in my back yard; therefore, a lot of our shopping was done at free clothing stores or at Goodwill. However, the good thing about that is nothing is ever too much money, so I could get whatever I liked. I was not always the happiest to go because my mom, Kathy M. Jones, looked at everything in the store twice. Sometime it seemed like we would have my next birthday while Mom was still looking around. Despite my better judgment, one Saturday I went with mom to the free place. I came in with my head down, knowing that I was going to waste my Saturday in this store and walking around like I had lost my best friend. Then I saw the most amazing thing my little five-year-old eyes had ever seen: a pair of brown cowboy boots with a black sole and white design on the sides. They were my rite of passage into the cowboy kingdom. I ran over and picked them up as fast as I could, knowing that if I was a second later, someone else was going to get them because who in the world would give up the chance to be a cowboy? I sat down and ripped my old shoes off with the same fury as a lion ripping into his prey. I slid the boots over my feet, and they fit like a glove and made me two inches taller. In addition, being the smallest of four sons, the boots made me feel less like an oompa loompa, a little green man running around singing songs in a Willy Wonka movie.

The love affair began, but remember that these were used boots the day I got them. They looked as if I had them for years and smelled like it too, but I looked past all that because of my dream of being a cowboy. I remember sleeping with them and trying to take a bath with them. I wore them with everything. It did not matter if I had shorts on or pants; I was wearing my boots. Obviously, I was going to wear them to school. That next day, I walked into my class smiling from ear to ear, knowing I was the new John Wayne in town. My entire class loved them, but there will always be haters.

My mom hated those boots with all her heart. My mom said they smelled like something died in them and then was left to rot. She told me they were ugly and they belonged in the trash. The battle began over the boots, and I was going to win. Mom was always trying to put them in the trash. In my mind, I was winning the battle of the boots because I still had them, and Mom had been trying to get them for months. Being so young, I did not know that battles can be won, but it is not over till you win the war. I guess all good things must come to an end, and one night my mom was that end. She somehow got the boots off me when I was sleeping. Truly, in this case, Mom won the War. My little cowboy heart was broken, so with a lost dream and broken imagination, my cowboy days came to an end. It is 20 years later, and I just got some more boots. My wife got these boots for me. However, I only wear them when I start feeling my inner cowboy crying to get out. Unfortunately for my wife, my inner cowboy cries a lot, and I can see a war coming. For now, all is well in the cowboy kingdom, and I still am John Wayne even if it is just in my mind.

By Daniel Yancey

Instructor: Dr. Marjorie Keil
Took Basic Writing: Fall 2010
Major: Business Administration
Advice: "Never think that you can't accomplish what you put your mind to."

Questions to Inspire Writing

1. Dan loved his cowboy boots. Describe your prized possession (past or present) and explain how much it means to you.

2. Dan's mom threw away his stinky boots. Did you ever have something you loved taken away? What happened? How did you handle your loss?

3. Did you have a vivid imagination as a child? What was your imaginary experience like?

4. As a child, what did you dream of "becoming" when you grew up? Now, what do you dream of becoming?

5. Write about your favorite TV show, movie, etc. and explain what you like and why you like it.

6. Write about your favorite activity/experience with a family member.

7. Write about the "most amazing thing" you've ever seen.

8. Do you have a "lost dream?" Does anyone close to you have a lost dream? Why did or didn't it "come true?" How have things worked out?

9. Wearing cowboy boots made Daniel feel like John Wayne, star of classic Western movies. Have you ever felt like a celebrity or the center of attention?

10. Have you ever felt like something you loved was taken away from you? Why? What do you now think about the reasons it was taken away? What were the outcomes?

11. What was going through your mind when you read this?

Donald M. Murray (1924–   ), professor, journalist, editor, writer, and television book reviewer, was born on September 16 in Boston. He earned the A.B. degree from the University of New Hampshire in 1948, attended Boston University, and served in the Airborne Division of the U.S. Army during World War II. A member of the National Council of Teachers of English and American Association of University Professors, Murray won the New England award from the Associated Press in 1951 and the Pulitzer Prize for editorial writing in 1954. Also a former writer for the *Boston Herald* and contributing editor to *Time,* Murray is a professor at the University of New Hampshire. His writings include A *Writer Teaches Writing: A Practical Method of Teaching Composition* (1968; 2d ed. 1985), *Learning by Teaching: Selected Articles on Writing and Teaching* (1982), *Writing for Your Readers* (1983), *Write to Learn* (1984), and *Read to Write* (1985). Murray has also written textbooks and novels.

The Maker's Eye: Revising Your Own Manuscripts

Donald M. Murray

When students complete a first draft, they consider the job of writing done—and their teachers too often agree. When professional writers complete a first draft, they usually feel that they are at the start of the writing process. When a draft is completed, the job of writing can begin.   1

That difference in attitude is the difference between amateur and professional, inexperience and experience, journeyman and craftsman. Peter F. Drucker, the prolific business writer, calls his first draft "the zero draft"—after that he can start counting. Most writers share the feeling that the first draft, and all of those which follow, are opportunities to discover what they have to say and how best they can say it.   2

To produce a progression of drafts, each of which says more and says it more clearly, the writer has to develop a special kind of reading skill. In school we are taught to decode what appears on the page as finished writing. Writers, however, face a different category of possibility and responsibility when they read their own drafts. To them the words on the page are never finished. Each can be changed and rearranged, can set off a chain reaction of confusion or clarified meaning. This is a different kind of reading which is possibly more difficult and certainly more exciting.   3

Writers must learn to be their own best enemy. They must accept the criticism of others and be suspicious of it; they must accept the praise of others and be even more suspicious of it. Writers cannot depend on others. They must detach themselves from their own pages so that they can apply both their caring and their craft to their own work.   4

Such detachment is not easy. Science fiction writer Ray Bradbury supposedly puts each manuscript away for a year to the day and then rereads it as a stranger. Not many writers have the discipline or the time to do this. We must read when our judgment may be at its worst, when we are close to the euphoric moment of creation.   5

Then the writer, counsels novelist Nancy Hale, "should be critical of everything that seems to him most delightful in his style. He should excise what he most admires, because he wouldn't thus admire it if he weren't . . . in a sense protecting it from criticism." John Ciardi, the poet, adds, "The last act of the writing must be to become one's own reader. It is, I suppose, a schizophrenic process, to begin passionately and to end critically, to begin hot and to end cold; and, more important, to be passion-hot and critic-cold at the same time." 6

Most people think that the principal problem is that writers are too proud of what they have written. Actually, a greater problem for most professional writers is one shared by the majority of students. They are overly critical, think everything is dreadful, tear up page after page, never complete a draft, see the task as hopeless. 7

The writer must learn to read critically but constructively, to cut what is bad, to reveal what is good. Eleanor Estes, the children's book author, explains: "The writer must survey his work critically, cooly, as though he were a stranger to it. He must be willing to prune, expertly and hard-heartedly. At the end of each revision, a manuscript may look . . . worked over, torn apart, pinned together, added to, deleted from, words changed and words changed back. Yet the book must maintain its original freshness and spontaneity." 8

Most readers underestimate the amount of rewriting it usually takes to produce spontaneous reading. This is a great disadvantage to the student writer, who sees only a finished product and never watches the craftsman who takes the necessary step back, studies the work carefully, returns to the task, steps back, returns, steps back, again and again. Anthony Burgess, one of the most prolific writers in the English-speaking world, admits, "I might revise a page twenty times." Ronald Dahl, the popular children's writer, states, "By the time I'm nearing the end of a story, the first part will have been reread and altered and corrected at least 150 times. . . . Good writing is essentially rewriting. I am positive of this." 9

Rewriting isn't virtuous. It isn't something that ought to be done. It is simply something that most writers find they have to do to discover what they have to say and how to say it. It is a condition of the writer's life. 10

There are, however, a few writers who do little formal rewriting, primarily because they have the capacity and experience to create and review a large number of invisible drafts in their minds before they approach the page. And some writers slowly produce finished pages, performing all the tasks of revision simultaneously, page by page, rather than draft by draft. But it is still possible to see the sequence followed by most writers most of the time in rereading their own work. 11

Most writers scan their drafts first, reading as quickly as possible to catch the larger problems of subject and form, then move in closer and closer as they read and write, reread and rewrite. 12

The first thing writers look for in their drafts is *information*. They know that a good piece of writing is built from specific, accurate, and interesting information. The writer must have an abundance of information from which to construct a readable piece of writing. 13

Next writers look for *meaning* in the information. The specifics must build to a pattern of significance. Each piece of specific information must carry the reader toward meaning.

Writers reading their own drafts are aware of *audience*. They put themselves in the reader's situation and make sure that they deliver information which a reader wants to know or needs to know in a manner which is easily digested. Writers try to be sure that they anticipate and answer the questions a critical reader will ask when reading the piece of writing.

Writers make sure that the *form* is appropriate to the subject and the audience. Form, or genre, is the vehicle which carries meaning to the reader, but form cannot be selected until the writer has adequate information to discover its significance and an audience which needs or wants that meaning.

Once writers are sure the form is appropriate, they must then look at the *structure*, the order of what they have written. Good writing is built on a solid framework of logic, argument, narrative, or motivation which runs through the entire piece of writing and holds it together. This is the time when many writers find it most effective to outline as a way of visualizing the hidden spine by which the piece of writing is supported.

The element on which writers may spend a majority of their time is *development*. Each section of a piece of writing must be adequately developed. It must give readers enough information so that they are satisfied. How much information is enough? That's as difficult as asking how much garlic belongs in a salad. It must be done to taste, but most beginning writers underdevelop, underestimating the reader's hunger for information.

As writers solve development problems, they often have to consider questions of *dimension*. There must be a pleasing and effective proportion among all the parts of the piece of writing. There is a continual process of subtracting and adding to keep the piece of writing in balance.

Finally, writers have to listen to their own voices. *Voice* is the force which drives a piece of writing forward. It is an expression of the writer's authority and concern. It is what is between the words on the page, what glues the piece of writing together. A good piece of writing is always marked by a consistent, individual voice.

As writers read and reread, write and rewrite, they move closer and closer to the page until they are doing line-by-line editing. Writers read their own pages with infinite care. Each sentence, each line, each clause, each phrase, each word, each mark of punctuation, each section of white space between the type has to contribute to the clarification of meaning.

Slowly the writer moves from word to word, looking through language to see the subject. As a word is changed, cut, or added, as a construction is rearranged, all the words used before that moment and all those that follow that moment must be considered and reconsidered.

Writers often read aloud at this stage of the editing process, muttering or whispering to themselves, calling on the ear's experience with language. Does this sound right—or that? Writers edit, shifting back and forth from eye to page to ear to page. I find I must do this careful editing in short runs, no more than fifteen or twenty minutes at a stretch, or I become too kind with myself. I begin to see what I hope is on the page, not what actually is on the page.

This sounds tedious if you haven't done it, but actually it is fun. Making something right is immensely satisfying, for writers begin to learn what they are writing about by writing. Language leads them to meaning, and there is the joy of discovery, of understanding, of making meaning clear as the writer employs the technical skills of language. 24

Words have double meanings, even triple and quadruple meanings. Each word has its own potential for connotation and denotation. And when writers rub one word against the other, they are often rewarded with a sudden insight, an unexpected clarification. 25

The maker's eye moves back and forth from word to phrase to sentence to paragraph to sentence to phrase to word. The maker's eye sees the need for variety and balance, for a firmer structure, for a more appropriate form. It peers into the interior of the paragraph, looking for coherence, unity, and emphasis, which make meaning clear. 26

I learned something about this process when my first bifocals were prescribed. I had ordered a larger section of the reading portion of the glass because of my work, but even so, I could not contain my eyes within this new limit of vision. And I still find myself taking off my glasses and bending my nose towards the page, for my eyes unconsciously flick back and forth across the page, back to another page, forward to still another, as I try to see each evolving line in relation to every other line. 27

When does this process end? Most writers agree with the great Russian writer Tolstoy, who said, "I scarcely ever reread my published writings, if by chance I come across a page, it always strikes me: all this must be rewritten; this is how I should have written it." 28

The maker's eye is never satisfied, for each word has the potential to ignite new meaning. This article has been twice written all the way through the writing process, and it was published four years ago. Now it is to be republished in a book. The editors make a few small suggestions, and then I read it with my maker's eye. Now it has been re-edited, re-revised, re-read, re-re-edited, for each piece of writing to the writer is full of potential and alternatives. 29

A piece of writing is never finished. It is delivered to a deadline, torn out of the typewriter on demand, sent off with a sense of accomplishment and shame and pride and frustration. If only there were a couple more days, time for just another run at it, perhaps then . . . 30

Questions for Discussion

1. How does Murray distinguish between drafting and writing? Why does he make this distinction?
2. What is Murray's implied criticism of the educational system, especially with how writing is taught?
3. What are the different kinds of drafts in the writing process? Which kinds do you use?
4. What should you be doing when you work on a college essay, according to Murray? What advice does he give for acquiring the skills necessary to do well?

5. What is voice? Can you be more specific than Murray? How do your classmates and teacher define voice?
6. Why does Murray call it a "maker's eye"?
7. Why might Murray have included quotes from many professional writers?

Questions for Reflection and Writing

1. Describe the writing process you use—in general or for a specific type of writing.
2. Analyze the voice and form of one of your own already written pieces—nonfiction, fiction, or poetry. Identify and label the techniques you used. What additional techniques could you have used?
3. Research the writing process of a writer you admire. Get information from biographies, articles, and published interviews.

Learning to Write

Russell Baker

► **PREREADING: BACKGROUND**

Virginia-born journalist Russell Baker began his career as London correspondent for the *Baltimore Sun.* In 1962, he began his widely syndicated "Observer" column for *The New York Times,* and in 1979 he received the Pulitzer Prize for distinguished commentary.

In "Learning to Write," Baker recalls his eleventh grade English class. He expected a dreary year with prim Mr. Fleagle, but things did not go entirely as he thought they would. Could Mr. Fleagle inspire after all? You decide as you read Baker's account of a life-altering event that occurred in a most unlikely place.

► **PREREADING: QUESTIONS**

1. How much writing did you do in high school?
2. What kind of writing assignments were you given?
3. Did you enjoy writing? Why or why not?
4. Did you ever discover you were good at something? If so, how?

► **HELPFUL DEFINITIONS**

notorious (1)—widely known
prim (1)—stiff and formal
listless (2)—without interest
fcrocity (2)—fierceness
irrepressible (2)—uncontrollable
antecedent (4)—the noun a pronoun replaces
reminiscence (8)—a written memory
repress (10)—hold back

Learning to Write

Russell Baker

1   When our class was assigned to Mr. Fleagle for third-year English I anticipated another grim year in that dreariest of subjects. Mr. Fleagle was notorious among City students for dullness and inability to inspire. He was said to be stuffy, dull, and hopelessly out of date. To me he looked to be sixty or seventy and prim to a fault. He wore primly severe eyeglasses, his wavy hair was primly cut and primly against the collar buttons of his primly starched white shirts. He had a primly pointed jaw, a primly straight nose, and a prim manner of speaking that was so correct, so gentlemanly, that he seemed a comic antique.

2   I anticipated a listless, unfruitful year with Mr. Fleagle and for a long time was not disappointed. We read *Macbeth*. Mr. Fleagle loved *Macbeth* and wanted us to love it too, but he lacked the gift of infecting others with his own passion. He tried to convey the murderous ferocity of Lady Macbeth one day by reading aloud the passage that concludes

> ...I have given suck, and now
> How tender 'tis to love the babe that milks me.
> I would, while it was smiling in my face,
> Have plucked my nipple from his boneless gums...

The idea of prim Mr. Fleagle plucking his nipple from boneless gums was too much for the class. We burst into gasps of irrepressible snickering. Mr. Fleagle stopped.

3   "There is nothing funny, boys, about giving suck to a babe. It is the—the very essence of motherhood, don't you see."

4   He constantly sprinkled his sentences with "don't you see." It wasn't a question but an exclamation of mild surprise at our ignorance. "Your pronoun needs an antecedent, don't you see," he would say, very primly. "The purpose of the Porter's scene, boys, is to provide comic relief from the horror, don't you see."

5   Late in the year we tackled the informal essay. "The essay, don't you see, is the..." My mind went numb. Of all forms of writing, none seemed so boring as the essay. Naturally we would have to write informal essays. Mr. Fleagle distributed a homework sheet offering us a choice of topics. None was quite so simpleminded as "What I Did on My Summer Vacation," but most seemed to be almost as dull. I took the list home and dawdled until the night before the essay was due. Sprawled on the sofa, I finally faced up to the grim task, took the list out of my notebook, and scanned it. The topic on which my eye stopped was "The Art of Eating Spaghetti."

6   This title produced an extraordinary sequence of mental images. Surging up out of the depths of memory came a vivid recollection of a night in Belleville when all of us were seated around the supper table Uncle Allen, my mother, Uncle Charlie, Uncle Hal—and Aunt Pat served spaghetti for supper. Spaghetti was an exotic treat in those days. Neither Doris nor I had ever eaten spaghetti, and none of the adults had enough experience to be good at it. All the good humor of Uncle Allen's house reawoke in my mind as I recalled the laughing arguments we had that night about the socially respectable method for moving spaghetti from plate to mouth.

7   Suddenly I wanted to write about that, about the warmth and good feeling of it, but I wanted to put it down simply for my own joy, not for Mr. Fleagle. It was a moment I wanted to recapture and hold for myself. I wanted to relive the pleasure of an evening at New Street. To write it as I wanted, however, would violate all the rules of formal composition I'd learned in school, and Mr. Fleagle would surely give it a failing grade. Never mind. I would write something else for Mr. Fleagle after I had written this thing for myself.

8   When I finished it the night was half gone and there was no time left to compose a proper, respectable essay for Mr. Fleagle. There was no choice next morning, but to turn in my private reminiscence of Belleville. Two days passed before Mr. Fleagle returned the graded papers, and he returned everyone's but mine. I was bracing myself for a command to report to Mr. Fleagle immediately after school for discipline when I saw him lift my paper from his desk and rap for the class's attention.

9   "Now, boys", he said, "I want to read you an essay. This is titled 'The Art of Eating Spaghetti.'"

10   And he started to read. My words! He was reading *my words* out loud to the entire class. What's more, the entire class was listening. Listening attentively. Then somebody laughed, then the entire class was laughing, and not in contempt and ridicule, but with openhearted enjoyment. Even Mr. Fleagle stopped two or three times to repress a small prim smile.

11   I did my best to avoid showing pleasure, but what I was feeling was pure ecstasy at this startling demonstration that my words had the power to make people laugh. In the eleventh grade, at the eleventh hour as it werc, I had discovered a calling. It was the happiest moment of my entire school career. When Mr. Fleagle finished he put the final seal on my happiness by saying, "Now that, boys, is an essay, don't you see. It's—don't you see—it's of the very essence of the essay, don't you see. Congratulations, Mr. Baker."

---

1. Do you think Mr. Fleagle was a good teacher? Explain why or why not.

2 In paragraph 7, Baker says that writing the essay the way he wanted to "would violate all the rules of formal composition [he'd] learned in school, and Mr. Fleagle would surely give it a failing grade." What do you think Baker is saying about writing classes and the kinds of writing done in them? Do you agree with Baker's assessment? Why or why not?

3. At first, Baker was not interested in writing an essay, but he soon changed his mind. Why?

4. What advice does your answer to number 3 suggest for writing teachers?

► QUESTIONS ON TECHNIQUE

1. Why do you think Baker describes Mr. Fleagle's primness in such detail (paragraph 1)? Why do you think Baker notes Mr. Fleagle's habit of saying "don't you see" (paragraph 4)?

2. To keep their stories lively and thereby hold their readers' interest, writers often use specific words. Thus, rather than use *shoe*, a writer might use the more specific *Nike hightop*, rather than use *walk*, a writer might use the more specific *stroll*. Baker uses specific words in "Learning to Write." For example in paragraph 5, he writes *scanned* rather than *looked at*. Cite four other examples of specific word choice.

3. A writer often tells a story because it has a particular significance. The significance of Baker's story is given in the last paragraph. Why do you think Baker mentions the significance there, rather than in paragraph 1?

4. In your own words, write a sentence that expresses the thesis of "Learning to Write." Which sentence in the essay comes closest to expressing that thesis idea?

► JOURNAL ENTRY

Using the information in "Learning to Write" and your own classroom experience for ideas, write a page or two of advice for high school teachers. Try to be specific. For example, rather than say, "Don't dress primly like Mr. Fleagle," offer a specific suggestion like "try dressing in sweaters to seem casual and approachable, but avoid jeans so you do not look like you want to be one of the students."

Baker uses conversation several times in his essay. With two or three classmates, discuss what that conversation contributes. What would the essay be like without it? For example, what difference would it make if paragraph 9 read like this: Mr. Fleagle told the class that he wanted to read an essay with the title "The Art of Eating Spaghetti?"

► WRITING TOPICS

1. Tell about the best or worst teacher you have had. Like Baker does in paragraphs 1–5, describe the teacher and use conversation to reveal something about his or her effectiveness in the classroom. Also, be sure your reader understands why the teacher was so good or bad. As an alternative, tell about the best or worst class you have had.

2. Compare and/or contrast a teacher you have had to Mr. Fleagle. Do both teachers have positive and negative qualities? Be sure to include examples or stories from both the reading and your own experience.

3. In eleventh grade, Russell Baker felt "pure ecstasy" (paragraph 11) when he learned he could use writing to make people laugh. Explain how you feel about writing and why you feel the way you do.

4. Tell a story about a happy or unhappy moment in your school career. In addition to telling what happened, explain the effect the moment had on you.

5. Baker expected junior English to be "another grim year" (paragraph 1). However, things did not go as he expected because he experienced "the happiest moment of [his] entire school career" (paragraph 11). Tell about a time when things did not go as you expected. Be sure to explain both what you expected and what actually happened.

Salvation

Langston Hughes

▶ PREREADING: BACKGROUND

Langston Hughes studied at Columbia University in New York in 1922, leaving after a year to travel to Africa and Europe. An important literary figure in the Harlem Renaissance, he has written not only his autobiography but also poetry, fiction, and children's books.

In the following narrative essay Hughes recalls a time when he experienced a great deal of pressure. How well did he cope with that pressure? You decide if he did the right thing as you read "Salvation."

▶ PREREADING: QUESTIONS

1. Have you ever been pressured by your family or peers into doing something that you didn't want to do?
2. Can you think of situations when lying is acceptable, or is it always wrong?
3. What role does religion play in your life?

▶ HELPFUL DEFINITIONS

revival (1)—emotional religious meeting
work-gnarled (4)—knotted from hard labor
rounder's (6)—belonging to an irresponsible wanderer
deacons (6)—church officers
serenely (7)—calmly
knickerbockered (11)—having shorts gathered at the knees
ecstatic (14)—emotional

Salvation

Langston Hughes

1   I was saved from sin when I was going on thirteen. But not really saved. It happened like this. There was a big revival at my Auntie Reed's church. Every night for weeks there had been much preaching, singing, praying, and shouting, and some very hardened sinners had been brought to Christ, and the membership of the church had grown by leaps and bounds. Then just before the revival ended, they held a special meeting for children, "to bring the young lambs to the fold." My aunt spoke of it for days ahead. That night I was escorted to the front row and placed on the mourners' bench with all the other young sinners, who had not yet been brought to Jesus.

2   My aunt told me that when you were saved you saw a light, and something happened to you inside! And Jesus came into your life! And God was with you from then on! She said you could see and hear and feel Jesus in your soul. I believed her. I had heard a great many old people say the same thing and it seemed to me they ought to know. So I sat there calmly in the hot, crowded church, waiting for Jesus to come to me.

3   The preacher preached a wonderful rhythmical sermon, all moans and shouts and lonely cries and dire pictures of hell, and then he sang a song about the ninety and nine safe in the fold, but one little lamb was left out in the cold. Then he said: "Won't you come? Won't you come to Jesus? Young lambs, won't you come?" And he held out his arms to all us young sinners there on the mourners' bench. And the little girls cried. And some of them jumped up and went to Jesus right away. But most of us just sat there.

4   A great many old people came and knelt around us and prayed, old women with jet-black faces and braided hair, old men with work-gnarled hands. And the church sang a song about the lower lights are burning, some poor sinners to be saved. And the whole building rocked with prayer and song.

5   Still I kept waiting to *see* Jesus.

6   Finally all the young people had gone to the altar and were saved, but onc boy and me. He was a rounder's son named Westley. Westley and I were surrounded by sisters and deacons praying. It was very hot in the church, and getting late now. Finally Westley said to me in a whisper: "God damn! I'm tired o' sitting here. Let's get up and be saved." So he got up and was saved.

7   Then I was left all alone on the mourners' bench. My aunt came and knelt at my knees and cried, while prayers and song swirled all around me in the little church. The whole congregation prayed for me alone, in a mighty wail of moans and voices. And I kept waiting serenely for Jesus, waiting, waiting—but he didn't come. I wanted to see him, but nothing happened to me. Nothing! I wanted something to happen to me, but nothing happened.

8   I heard the songs and the minister saying: "Why don't you come? My dear child, why don't you come to Jesus? Jesus is waiting for you. He want you. Why don't you come? Sister Reed, what is this child's name?"

9   "Langston," my aunt sobbed.

10 "Langston, why don't you come? Why don't you come and be saved? Oh, Lamb of God! Why don't you come?"

11 Now it was really getting late. I began to be ashamed of myself, holding everything up so long. I began to wonder what God thought about Westley, who certainly hadn't seen Jesus either, but who was now sitting proudly on the platform, swinging his knickerbockered legs and grinning down at me, surrounded by deacons and old women on their knees praying. God had not struck Westley dead for taking his name in vain or for lying in the temple. So I decided that maybe to save further trouble, I'd better lie, too, and say that Jesus had come, and get up and be saved.

12 So I got up.

13 Suddenly the whole room broke into a sea of shouting, as they saw me rise. Waves of rejoicing swept the place. Women leaped in the air. My aunt threw her arms around me. The minister took me by the hand and led me to the platform.

14 When things quieted down, in a hushed silence, punctuated by a few ecstatic "Amens," all the new young lambs were blessed in the name of God. Then joyous singing filled the room.

15 That night, for the last time in my life but one—for I was a big boy twelve years old—I cried. I cried, in bed alone, and couldn't stop. I buried my head under the quilts, but my aunt heard me. She woke up and told my uncle I was crying because the Holy Ghost had come into my life, and because I had seen Jesus. But I was really crying because I couldn't bear to tell her that I had lied, that I had deceived everybody in the church, that I hadn't seen Jesus, and that now I didn't believe there was a Jesus any more, since he didn't come to help me.

▶ **QUESTIONS ON CONTENT**

1. What do you think Hughes's aunt means when she speaks of seeing and hearing Jesus? Does she *literally* see and hear him? What do you think Hughes thinks she means?

2. What do you think Hughes is waiting for?

3. Why does Hughes finally lie, saying he is saved? Do you think he did the right thing by lying?

4. At the end of the story, Hughes goes home to bed and cries. Why?

▶ QUESTIONS ON TECHNIQUE

1. When writers use *irony*, they express the opposite of what they really mean. For example, in paragraph 1, Hughes does not really think that the people at the revival were "hardened sinners." Where else in the essay does Hughes use irony?

2. To make a story come alive for a reader, an author sometimes uses descriptive words and phrases that appeal to the senses (sight, sound, taste, smell, and touch). For example, in paragraph 4, Hughes refers to "old women with jet-black faces and braided hair. . . ." Cite four other examples of descriptive language that helps the story come alive.

3. Do the opening two sentences stimulate your interest and make you want to read on? Why or why not?

▶ JOURNAL ENTRY

Hughes's essay describes a childhood experience that had a significant impact on his view of his religion and himself. List experiences that have changed your attitude or opinion or that have made you see things in a new way.

▶ COLLABORATIVE ACTIVITY

When telling a story, writers often use time transitions—words and phrases that indicate time order. For example, in paragraph 6, Hughes writes, "Finally all the young people had gone to the altar. . . ." *Finally* indicates the last event in a time sequence. With two or three classmates, go through the essay and find other time transitions.

▶ WRITING TOPICS

1. Religion has a different meaning for Hughes and his aunt. Write about the role of religion in your life or in the life of someone close to you, perhaps telling how that role changed over the years.

2. Young people face many pressures as they grow to adulthood. Identify one or two of those pressures and explain positive ways young people might cope with them.

3. Write about one of the experiences that you compiled in your journal

entry. Be sure to tell the story and also discuss how the experience affected you.

4. Have you ever found yourself in an uncomfortable or even potentially dangerous situation because you were pressured into it? Tell about the event and how you dealt with it. Be sure to also explain what you learned from the situation.

Just Walk on By: A Black Man Ponders His Power to Alter Public Space

Brent Staples

▶ **PREREADING: BACKGROUND**

Brent Staples was raised with eight brothers and sisters in Chester, Pennsylvania, and attended graduate school at the University of Chicago. An editor and writer for the *New York Times,* Staples is also the author of *Parallel Time: Growing Up in Black and White* (1994). In the following essay, originally published in *MS Magazine* in 1986, Staples explains that because other people find his appearance threatening, he, himself, is at risk.

▶ **PREREADING: QUESTIONS**

1. How often do you judge people by their appearance?
2. Have you ever been judged by the way you looked? How did you feel about this?
3. Are you afraid or nervous around people you do not know? Why or why not?
4. What do you think "alter public space" means?

▶ **HELPFUL DEFINITIONS**

affluent (1)—wealthy
discreet (1)—cautious, prudent
dicey (2)—risky, dangerous
errant(2)—incorrect, wrong
SoHo (4)—a section of New York City, an artistic community
bandolier (6)—ammunition belt worn across the chest
solace (6)—comfort
in retrospect (7)—looking back, reviewing the past
bravado (9)—false courage
labyrinthine (10)—resembling a maze

Just Walk on By: A Black Man Ponders His Power to Alter Public Space

Brent Staples

1   My first victim was a woman—white, well dressed, probably in her early twenties. I came upon her late one evening on a deserted street in Hyde Park, a relatively affluent neighborhood in an otherwise mean, impoverished section of Chicago. As I swung onto the avenue behind her, there seemed to be a discreet, uninflammatory distance between us. Not so. She cast back a worried glance. To her, the youngish black man—a broad six feet two inches with a beard and billowing hair, both hands shoved into the pockets of a bulky military jacket—seemed menacingly close. After a few more quick glimpses, she picked up her pace and was soon running in earnest. Within seconds she disappeared into a cross street.

2   That was more than a decade ago. I was 22 years old, a graduate student newly arrived at the University of Chicago. It was in the echo of that terrified woman's footfalls that I first began to know the unwieldy inheritance I'd come into—the ability to alter public space in ugly ways. It was clear that she thought herself the quarry of a mugger, a rapist, or worse. Suffering a bout of insomnia, however, I was stalking sleep, not defenseless wayfarers. As a softy who is scarcely able to take a knife to a raw chicken—let alone hold it to a person's throat—I was surprised, embarrassed, and dismayed all at once. Her flight made me feel like an accomplice in tyranny. It also made it clear that I was indistinguishable from the muggers who occasionally seeped into the area from the surrounding ghetto. That first encounter, and those that followed, signified that a vast, unnerving gulf lay between nighttime pedestrians—particularly women—and me. And I soon gathered that being perceived as dangerous is a hazard in itself. I only needed to turn a corner into a dicey situation, or crowd some frightened, armed person in a foyer somewhere, or make an errant move after being pulled over by a policeman. Where fear and weapons meet—and they often do in urban America—there is always the possibility of death.

3   In that first year, my first away from my hometown, I was to become thoroughly familiar with the language of fear. At dark, shadowy intersections in Chicago, I could cross in front of a car stopped at a traffic light and elicit the *thunk, thunk, thunk, thunk* of the driver—black, white, male,

or female—hammering down the door locks. On less traveled streets after dark, I grew accustomed to but never comfortable with people who crossed to the other side of the street rather than pass me. Then there were the standard unpleasantries with police, doormen, bouncers, cab drivers, and others whose business it is to screen out troublesome individuals *before* there is any nastiness.

4   I moved to New York nearly two years ago and I have remained an avid night walker. In central Manhattan, the near constant crowd cover minimizes tense one-on-one street encounters. Elsewhere—visiting friends in SoHo, where sidewalks are narrow and tightly spaced buildings shut out the sky—things can get very taut indeed.

5   Black men have a firm place in New York mugging literature. Norman Podhoretz in his famed (or infamous) 1963 essay, "My Negro Problem—And Ours," recalls growing up in terror of black males; they "were tougher than we were, more ruthless," he writes—and as an adult on the Upper West Side of Manhattan, he continues, he cannot constrain his nervousness when he meets black men on certain streets. Similarly, a decade later, the essayist and novelist Edward Hoagland extols a New York where once "Negro bitterness bore down mainly on other Negroes." Where some see mere panhandlers, Hoagland sees "a mugger who is clearly screwing up his nerve to do more than just *ask* for money." But Hoagland has "the New Yorker's quick-hunch posture for broken-field maneuvering," and the bad guy swerves away.

6   I often witness that "hunch posture," from women after dark on the warrenlike streets of Brooklyn where I live. They seem to set their faces on neutral and, with their purse straps strung across their chests bandolier style, they forge ahead as though bracing themselves against being tackled. I understand, of course, that the danger they perceive is not a hallucination. Women are particularly vulnerable to street violence, and young black males are drastically overrepresented among the perpetrators of that violence. Yet these truths are no solace against the kind of alienation that comes of being ever the suspect, against being set apart, a fearsome entity with whom pedestrians avoid making eye contact.

7   It is not altogether clear to me how I reached the ripe old age of 22 without being consciousof the lethality nighttime pedestrians attributed to me. Perhaps it was because in Chester, Pennsylvania, the small, angry industrial town where I came of age in the 1960s, I was scarcely noticeable against a backdrop of gang warfare, street knifings, and murders. I grew up one of the good boys, had perhaps a half-dozen fist fights. In retrospect, my shyness of combat has clear sources.

8   Many things go into the making of a young thug. One of those things is the consummation of the male romance with the power to intimidate. An infant discovers that random flailings send the baby bottle flying out of the crib and crashing to the floor. Delighted, the joyful babe repeats

those motions again and again, seeking to duplicate the feat. Just so, I recall the points at which some of my boyhood friends were finally seduced by the perception of themselves as tough guys. When a mark cowered and surrendered his money without resistance, myth and reality merged—and paid off. It is, after all, only manly to embrace the power to frighten and intimidate. We, as men, are not supposed to give an inch of our lane on the highway; we are to seize the fighter's edge in work and in play and even in love; we are to be valiant in the face of hostile forces.

9   Unfortunately, poor and powerless young men seem to take all this nonsense literally. As a boy, I saw countless tough guys locked away; I have since buried several, too. They were babies really—a teenage cousin, a brother of 22, a childhood friend in his mid-twenties—all gone down in episodes of bravado played out in the streets. I came to doubt the virtues of intimidation early on. I chose, perhaps even unconsciously, to remain a shadow—timid, but a survivor.

10   The fearsomeness mistakenly attributed to me in public places often has a perilous flavor. The most frightening of these confusions occurred in the late 1970s and early 1980s when I worked as a journalist in Chicago. One day, rushing into the office of a magazine I was writing for with a deadline story in hand, I was mistaken for a burglar. The office manager called security and, with an ad hoc posse, pursued me through the labyrinthine halls, nearly to my editor's door. I had no way of proving who I was. I could only move briskly toward the company of someone who knew me.

11   Another time I was on assignment for a local paper and killing time before an interview. I entered a jewelry store on the city's affluent Near North Side. The proprietor excused herself and returned with an enormous red Doberman pinscher straining at the end of a leash. She stood, the dog extended toward me, silent to my questions, her eyes bulging nearly out of her head. I took a cursory look around, nodded, and bade her good night. Relatively speaking, however, I never fared as badly as another black male journalist. He went to nearby Waukegan, Illinois, a couple of summers ago to work on a story about a murderer who was born there. Mistaking the reporter for the killer, police hauled him from his car at gunpoint and but for his press credentials would probably have tried to book him. Such episodes are not uncommon. Black men trade tales like this all the time.

12   In "My Negro Problem—And Ours," Podhoretz writes that the hatred he feels for blacks makes itself known to him through a variety of avenues—one being his discomfort with that "special brand of paranoid touchiness" to which he says blacks are prone. No doubt he is speaking here of black men. In time, I learned to smother the rage I felt at so often being taken for a criminal. Not to do so would surely have led to madness—via that special "paranoid touchiness" that so annoyed Podhoretz at the time he wrote the essay.

13   I began to take precautions to make myself less threatening. I move about with care, particularly late in the evening. I give a wide berth to nervous people on subway platforms during the wee hours, particularly when I have exchanged business clothes for jeans. If I happen to be entering a building behind some people who appear skittish, I may walk by, letting them clear the lobby before I return, so as not to seem to be following them. I have been calm and extremely congenial on those rare occasions when I've been pulled over by the police.

14   And on late evening constitutionals along streets less traveled by, I employ what has proved to be an excellent tension-reducing measure: I whistle melodies from Beethoven and Vivaldi and the more popular classical composers. Even steely New Yorkers hunching toward nighttime destinations seem to relax, and occasionally they even join in the tune. Virtually everybody seems to sense that a mugger wouldn't be warbling bright, sunny selections from Vivaldi's *Four Seasons*. It is my equivalent of the cowbell that hikers wear when they know they are in bear country.

▲

▶ **QUESTIONS ON CONTENT**

1. According to Staples, why is it a problem to be perceived as dangerous?

2. Does Staples believe that people's fear of young black men is legitimate? Explain.

3. According to the author, what causes young black males to lead violent lives? Why didn't Staples himself fall into a life of violence?

4. What do you think of Staples's personal solution to the problem of being perceived as dangerous?

▶ **QUESTIONS ON TECHNIQUE**

1. In your own words, write out the thesis (main point) of the essay. Which sentence in the essay best expresses that thesis?

2. When you read the opening two sentences, what did you think the essay would be about? Were your expectations fulfilled? Do you think these two sentences are a good opening strategy? Why or why not?

3. Which paragraphs use brief examples to illustrate a point? Which paragraphs use narration (storytelling) to illustrate a point?

4. What main contrast appears in the essay?

Based on your physical appearance (height, weight, manner of dress, skin color, and so forth) explain the impression a stranger would form after seeing you for the first time. How do you feel about that impression?

► COLLABORATIVE ACTIVITY

Young black males are not the only people judged by their appearance. With several classmates, make a list of groups who often are stereotyped because of how they look.

► WRITING TOPICS

1. Tell about a time when you were frightened by a person or a situation. Explain what caused the fear and how your behavior was influenced by it. As an alternative, tell about a time you frightened someone else. Explain what caused the fright and what the effects were.

2. Describe your first impression of someone. Explain why you formed that impression and whether or not it proved to be accurate.

3. Pick one of the following and explain how that person is likely to be perceived by others and how that perception affects the person. If you do not have firsthand knowledge, interview someone for information:

   a very tall person
   a very short person
   a very beautiful or handsome person
   a very muscular person
   a poorly dressed person
   a male with long hair
   a male with an earring
   a woman with blonde hair
   a physically disabled person
   a well-dressed person

4. In paragraph 8, Staples explains what goes into "the making of a young thug." He explains that it is "only manly to embrace the power to frighten and intimidate." As a result, Staples concludes, "We, as men, are not supposed to give an inch of our lane on the highway; we are to seize the fighter's edge in work and play and even in love; we are to be valiant in the face of hostile forces." Do you agree that this is how society interprets masculinity? Cite examples to support your view.

Daddy Tucked the Blanket

Randall Williams

▶ PREREADING: BACKGROUND

In this autobiographical essay, Randall Williams, a former reporter for *The Alabama Journal,* shares an unhappy part of his childhood. Using examples, he relates the impact that substandard housing had on his family, especially his parents.

▶ PREREADING: QUESTIONS

1. Does where you live affect who you are? Why or why not?
2. Do you remember a time in grade school when a child was treated cruelly by classmates because he or she was different in some way?
3. Did you ever feel the need to "get out" or escape from a family situation? How did you resolve the problem?

▶ HELPFUL DEFINITIONS

shiftless (7)—lazy, lacking ambition
articulate (7)—able to express oneself clearly
sweltering (9)—excessively hot
deteriorating (12)—worsening in quality
futility (13)—ineffectiveness, uselessness
psyche (20)—self, mind
affluent (21)—wealthy
retrospect (25)—review of past events

Daddy Tucked the Blanket

Randall Williams

1   About the time I turned 16, my folks began to wonder why I didn't stay home any more. I always had an excuse for them, but what I didn't say was that I had found my freedom and I was getting out.

2   I went through four years of high school in semirural Alabama and became active in clubs and sports; I made a lot of friends and became a regular guy, if you know what I mean. But one thing was irregular about me; I managed those four years without ever having a friend visit at my house.

3   I was ashamed of where I lived. I had been ashamed for as long as I had been conscious of class.

4   We had a big family. There were several of us sleeping in one room, but that's not so bad if you get along, and we always did. As you get older, though, it gets worse.

5   Being poor is a humiliating experience for a young person trying hard to be accepted. Even now—several years removed—it is hard to talk about. And I resent the weakness of these words to make you feel what it was really like.

6   We lived in a lot of old houses. We moved a lot because we were always looking for something just a little better than what we had. You have to understand that my folks worked harder than most people. My mother was always at home, but for her that was a full-time job—and no fun, either. But my father worked his head off from the time I can remember in construction and shops. It was hard, physical work.

7   I tell you this to show that we weren't shiftless. No matter how much money Daddy made, we never made much progress up the social ladder. I got out thanks to a college scholarship and because I was a little more articulate than the average.

8   I have seen my Daddy wrap copper wire through the soles of his boots to keep them together in the wintertime. He couldn't buy new boots because he had used the money for food and shoes for us. We lived like hell, but we went to school well-clothed and with a full stomach.

9   It really is hell to live in a house that was in bad shape 10 years before you moved in. And a big family puts a lot of wear and tear on a new house, too, so you can imagine how one goes downhill if it is teetering when you move in. But we lived in houses that were sweltering in summer and freezing in winter. I woke up every morning for a year and a half with plaster on my face where it had fallen out of the ceiling during the night.

10   This wasn't during the Depression; this was in the late 60's and early 70's.

11   When we boys got old enough to learn trades in school, we would try to fix up the old houses we lived in. But have you ever tried to paint a wall that crumbled when the roller went across it? And bright paint emphasized the holes in the wall. You end up more frustrated than when you began, especially when you know that at best you might come up with only enough money to improve one of the six rooms in the house. And we might move out soon after, anyway.

12   The same goes for keeping a house like that clean. If you have a house full of kids and the house is deteriorating, you'll never keep it clean. Daddy used to yell at Mama about that, but she couldn't do anything. I think Daddy knew it inside, but he had to have an outlet for his rage somewhere, and at least yelling isn't as bad as hitting, which they never did to each other.

13   But you have a kitchen which has no counter space and no hot water, and you will have dirty dishes stacked up. That sounds like an excuse, but try it. You'll go mad from sheer sense of futility. It's the same thing in a house with no closets. You can't keep clothes clean and rooms in order if they have to be stacked up with things.

14   Living in a bad house is generally worse on girls. For one thing, they traditionally help their mother with the housework. We boys could get outside and work in the field or cut wood or even play ball and forget about living conditions. The sky was still pretty.

15   But the girls got the pressure, and as they got older it became worse. Would they accept dates knowing they had to "receive" the young man in a dirty hallway with broken windows, peeling wallpaper and a cracked ceiling? You have to live it to understand it, but it creates a shame which drives the soul of a young person inward.

16   I'm thankful none of us ever blamed our parents for this, because it would have crippled our relationships. As it worked out, only the relationship between our parents was damaged. And I think the harshness which they expressed to each other was just an outlet to get rid of their anger at the trap their lives were in. It ruined their marriage because they had no one to yell at but each other. I knew other families where the kids got the abuse, but we were too much loved for that.

17   Once I was about 16 and Mama and Daddy had had a particularly violent argument about the washing machine, which had broken down. Daddy was on the back porch—that's where the only water faucet was—trying to fix it and Mama had a washtub out there washing school clothes for the next day and they were screaming at each other.

18   Later that night everyone was in bed and I heard Daddy get up from the couch where he was reading. I looked out from my bed across the hall into their room. He was standing right over Mama and she was already asleep. He pulled the blanket up and tucked it around her shoul-

ders and just stood there and tears were dropping off his cheeks and I thought I could faintly hear them splashing against the linoleum rug.

19 Now they're divorced.

20 I had courses in college where housing was discussed, but the sociologists never put enough emphasis on the impact living in substandard housing has on a person's psyche. Especially children's.

21 Small children have a hard time understanding poverty. They want the same things children from more affluent families have. They want the same things they see advertised on television, and they don't understand why they can't have them.

22 Other children can be incredibly cruel. I was in elementary school in Georgia—and this is interesting because it is the only thing I remember about that particular school—when I was about eight or nine.

23 After Christmas vacation had ended, my teacher made each student describe all his or her Christmas presents. I became more and more uncomfortable as the privilege passed around the room toward me. Other children were reciting the names of the dolls they had been given, the kinds of bicycles and the grandeur of their games and toys. Some had lists which seemed to go on and on for hours.

24 It took me only a few seconds to tell the class that I had gotten for Christmas a belt and a pair of gloves. And then I was laughed at—because I cried—by a roomful of children and a teacher. I never forgave them, and that night I made my mother cry when I told her about it.

25 In retrospect, I am grateful for that moment, but I remember wanting to die at the time.

▶ QUESTIONS ON CONTENT

1. Why do you think that Williams's family "never made much progress up the social ladder" (paragraph 7)?

2. Why do you think the author stresses the fact that his family wasn't "shiftless" (paragraph 7)?

3. Do you agree with Williams when he writes that "living in a bad house is generally worse on girls" (paragraph 14)? Explain.

4. Williams writes of being laughed at by his teacher and classmates when telling what presents he received for Christmas. Why do you think he feels "grateful for that moment" (paragraph 25)?

5 How do you think Williams finally escaped from poverty?

▶ QUESTIONS ON TECHNIQUE

1. Do you think "Daddy Tucked the Blanket" is a good title for this essay? Explain.

2. His word choice often makes Williams sound as if he is talking to the reader. For example, he writes, "If you know what I mean" (paragraph 2). Find three other examples of such word choice. Why do you think he speaks so directly to the reader?

3. Cite three times Williams uses examples to show the negative effects of poverty on his family and him.

4. Williams follows his lengthy description of his father tucking his mother in bed with a very short sentence: "Now they're divorced" (paragraph 19). What effect does such a short sentence create? Find another example of a relatively short sentence that follows a long one.

5. Why does Williams mention that "this wasn't during the Depression" (paragraph 10)?

▶ **JOURNAL ENTRY**

If money were no object, what kind of a house would you live in? Describe your dream house.

▶ **COLLABORATIVE ACTIVITY**

Williams notes that children want the things they see advertised on television and don't understand why they can't always have them. For poor children, this can be especially painful. What other negative effects does television have on people? In answering this question, you might consider, among other things, how news coverage, stereotypes, and sex on television shape our attitudes.

▶ **WRITING TOPICS**

1. Williams writes that "children can be incredibly cruel" (paragraph 22). Tell of an event that you or someone else experienced that proves this point. Be sure to discuss how you or that person was affected by the experience.

2. Williams's parents, like many modern parents, got divorced. Discuss the typical causes for divorce or the effects of divorce on a family.

3. If you and your family have ever moved into a new neighborhood, tell how the move affected you and your family.

4. Think of one aspect of your upbringing—for example, your family's views on discipline, politics, religion, or education; where you lived; where you attended school—and use examples to show how it affected you.

5. As Williams shows, where we live affects who we are. Write about the neighborhood or city where you grew up, showing through your use of examples how it shaped your attitudes and view of the world.

6. In paragraph 5, Williams notes that proverty is humiliating to a young person. Use examples to illustrate something else that is humiliating.

Index